EAT CAKE. BE BRAVE.

MELISSA RADKE

GRAND CENTRAL
PUBLISHING

New York   Boston

Grand Central Publishing
Hachette Book Group
1290 Avenue of the Americas, New York, NY 10104
grandcentralpublishing.com
twitter.com/grandcentralpub

First Edition: July 2018

Grand Central Publishing is a division of Hachette Book Group, Inc. The Grand Central Publishing name and logo is a trademark of Hachette Book Group, Inc.

The publisher is not responsible for websites (or their content) that are not owned by the publisher.

The Hachette Speakers Bureau provides a wide range of authors for speaking events. To find out more, go to www.hachettespeakersbureau.com or call (866) 376-6591.

Library of Congress Control Number: 2018939703

ISBNs: 978-1-5387-1216-0 (hardcover), 978-1-5387-1218-4 (ebook)

Printed in the United States of America

LSC-C

10 9 8 7 6 5 4 3 2 1

For my mom and my dad,
who have given everything they have to love
me, teach me, and make me... Brave.
Every bit of this, is you.

Contents

Contents

Contents

Preface

Hi. My name is Melissa Radke, and there is a very real chance you have no idea who I am. But trust me on this: *You are going to love me.*

Those are the exact words I said to my college roommate immediately upon meeting her the first day of freshman year. A few weeks later she would move to another hall because of my snoring and take three pairs of my sneakers with her. I hope you don't decide to do that. But if you do, *joke's on you, sucker,* because I don't wear sneakers anymore. Flat feet! *Boom!*

I wasn't planning on writing a preface to my own book. It seems gauche. I think prefaces are reserved for authors who have written a few best-selling books or been interviewed by Gayle King; authors who say things like:

"I wrote this in a cabin in the Andes, Gayle. I was snowed in for three months and had to forage for my own food."

"This book came to me after I came face-to-face with my own existential existence."

"Believe it or not, Gayle, I was having a root canal and I literally died in the chair. I saw heaven. And when I came back to earth I could speak Mandarin."

None of those happened for me.

Although if Gayle King were to ever ask me . . .

"I wrote this book between taking my kids to the local pool and picking out flip-flops at Old Navy. Did I ever have to forage for my own food? No, in fact, I ate my weight in chicken strips."

"This book came to me after I looked directly into one of those mirrors with the ten times magnification. Never, ever do that."

"I have never seen heaven, I have never experienced hell . . . *Oh wait, yes, I have!* At some point during writing chapter 5, I agreed to attend one of those ceramic paint parties with some of my friends. I would consider that *hell*."

So yeah, a preface, coming from me, seems brazen. I figure you should just turn the page and see for yourself whether we are going to be friends; you shouldn't just take me at my word—you should make me earn it.

But wait!

Before you do.

There are a few things about me that I want you to know first.

I have been married for twenty-three years at the writing of this book; seventeen of those have been awesome. I love David with all my heart even though he is dogmatic, authoritarian, imperious, dictatorial, uncompromising, unyielding, and unflexible. I call him the Attorney General, for he is full of rules and regulations, and no fun can be found in him at all. I mean, think about it, not once have you ever heard anyone say, "Hey! Let's have a party this weekend! Somebody call an attorney general and see if they can come; they're a lot of fun!" No. Instead you hear sentences like, "The state attorney general will be tried twice over charges of securities fraud and violation of federal securities regulations." Oh yeah...*now there's a party*. And yet, this year, when he surprised me with a vow renewal on a beach in Maui with our dearest friends, I said to him what I believe wholeheartedly to be true: *It's you, David Radke. It has always been you.* (But just in case he ever murders me: The reason is hidden in the fifth sentence of this preface.)

We have two children. Their names are Remi and Rocco. I want so badly to tell you that our children are named things like Charlotte after my great-grandmother who came over from Croatia to experience a New World, or Elkanah, which is a Hebrew word meaning "the zeal of God." But the truth is, we saw "Remi" stitched across the back of a child-size rocking chair that had been marked 40 percent off, and Rocco DiSpirito is a chef with pretty hair. I saw him on a reality show once. That's right. I make my choices based off reality TV and storewide discounts. I'm not proud of it. What I am proud of, though, are those two children. We waited a long time and fought hard for them. I have often said my children are my Purple Hearts: They are the reward that came to me after I took a wounding from the battle. And I would do it all again even if I knew it meant my Friday nights would be spent eating at Chick-fil-A, watching *Boss Baby*, and falling sound asleep at eight fifteen p.m. I would do every bit of it again. For them.

I come from a big-boned Southern family. We laugh really loudly, and we cook a whole lot. When you marry into our family you can be assured of these three things:

1. If you are shy or timid or quiet, it is registered as "non-love" and they will wonder why you hate them and won't speak to them and they will grieve over this until the day you finally decide to be as loud and obnoxious as they are, at which point they will whisper behind your back, "What's going on with the Attorney General? At first, he never spoke to us, and now he is so loud your mother couldn't hear the timer going off on the oven so her chicken and dressing turned out dry...I just don't understand what we could have done to make him hate us so much." You will never be able to figure this out. Don't try.

2. If you try to bring anything into our homes for a holiday get-together that is not homemade, you will be asked leave. That is all. They will not even discuss this with you.

3. If you are a female who has married into our family: Do not look better than we do in a bathing suit. Now, as you can imagine, this is tricky because we all look horrible in a bathing suit. But we need you to look horrible-er. Don't try to trick us by wearing a sarong over your swimsuit and saying it's because you gained weight. No! You will wear a swim dress and you will look awful in it.

I also want you to know that 97 percent of everything you read in this book is absolute truth. I cannot say 100 percent because I saw that *Oprah* episode where she questioned James Frey, and y'all, she lit that guy up! So, yeah, some of these things happened too many years ago, and I get gray on times or dates or surrounding events. I do not, however, get gray on my feelings. I am never gray on what is true to me. I remember what I felt. Isn't that always the way? We might not remember what they wore, but we remember how they made us feel small. So, I would just advise you to be careful how you treat people...they might just write a book someday.

I wrote this book for two people, and two people only. You and me.

I wrote it for me because when I turned forty-one I decided to be brave with my life. I decided to live differently than I ever had before. I have never jumped out of an airplane, I have never climbed Mount Everest, and do not even think about trying to get me down in one of those cages to see sharks. No, this was a different kind of bravery. It was the kind where I decided to live bolder and freer, unfettered by what moms are supposed to do or how middle-aged women should behave. It wasn't too late for me.

I would make sure of it.

No one's life is supposed to change at forty-one.

But mine did.

Mine changed drastically.

And I met it, courageously.

To the Very Serious Reader, and also to the woman who coincidentally came across this book in a bookstore somewhere and simply bought it because it had the word *cake* in it:

I wrote it for you. I spotted you, you know?

I spotted you waiting in line for the newest Reese Witherspoon movie.

I spotted you sitting in church or in the booth behind me at my favorite Mexican food place.

I saw you in line at the bank or in the pediatrician's office with a sick child.

I watched you serve drinks on a crowded flight and take tickets on opening night.

I passed you coming out of the bathroom at a Coldplay

concert, and I saw you order a coffee on a cold Monday morning.

I saw you shopping alone. I saw you teaching my children. I saw you taking their temperature.

I've seen you laugh when you didn't feel like it, and I've heard you cry when you wanted to scream, and I just wanted you to know—I just wanted to make absolutely sure you knew—you were seen. You were seen when the doctor's report was bleak, and you were seen when the papers were served. You were seen at your best, and you were seen at your worst.

When friends left and lovers cheated.

When lies were told and truth was distant.

You were not forgotten, looked over, or abandoned.

I am here today because you are one of God's personal favorites. As in, if He was having a huge get-together with loud music and friends and family, He would make sure you knew you were invited. He would refuse to even cut the cake until He knew you were in the house. There would be no toasts, no cheers, and He wouldn't dare let anyone even think about cranking up the music unless you were standing close by. And maybe, just maybe, it will take you reading about me finding my worth in order for you to finally believe in yours.

So, here's to bravery.

Here's to courage.

Here's to cake. (And not the crappy kind, like carrot.)

—Melissa

Chapter 1

A List of Things We Should Probably Get Out of the Way.

You know those things that travel around Facebook where you get to list various interesting things about yourself? It's kind of the adult version of an eighth grade slam book. *Y'all!* No one has ever asked me to do that. Nor have they begged or pleaded with me (when everyone knows that is *specifically* what I want). Not that you necessarily have to be asked—but it would be nice. A quick post with "Hey, Mel, I would love to hear your thoughts on yourself" never hurt anybody.

But never.

Not once.

Sometimes at the bottom of the post different people

will be tagged and it will say, "I now tag these four people because I know theirs will be awesome: Rhonda Brady, Kelli Hankins, April Willett, Kerri Mullins. Go for it, girls!" But no one has ever tagged me—and y'all, I'm starting to get whiny about it.

But who's laughing now? Because I've got myself a book, suckers! So, I'm going to dedicate an entire chapter to the oddities, abnormalities, and endearing qualities that make me, me.

Will this chapter change your life in any way? No, absolutely not.

Will it make you brave? No.

But it might make you want to eat cake. Or not. I don't know.

There is also the small chance it might make you feel a lot less weird and a lot more normal. Or it will make you look into therapy. Both are wins!

———⬥———

So here we go. A list of twenty-six things about me that will surprise some, intrigue none, and embarrass my mother.

1. I am a hands person. I determine whether I want to even get to know you by looking at your hands. I once had a meeting with one of the best business managers in all the land but it was a

firm no for me before the appetizers even arrived
when I saw his fingers looked like Twinkies. Interesting side note: My hands look like a polar
bear's paws. When I eat chicken, I look like a
bear that just wrestled its dinner out of a stream.
I'm not going to get over my hands issue, but I
am going to have to ask that you get over yours.

2. I cannot say the word *rewind*. I say *re-rind*. Don't
try to fix me. You cannot imagine my delight
when VCR tapes went out of fashion.

3. I once went to Sonic and asked the voice taking
my order if their wieners were all beef. He did
not answer me for twelve seconds. When he
came back, his reply was, "Yes, Mrs. Radke, Tim
says his wiener is definitely all beef and that
you'll love it." The saddest part of this story, I
am telling you, is that I went to church with
Tim's mom and should have called her right
then and told her about her child. But I didn't.
Because I was flattered. I ate there once a week
for two years.

4. I wrote Kirk Cameron a letter in the fourth
grade because I needed him to know I was in
love with him and that we shared a mutual love
of racquetball. I am guessing the reason he did
not write me back was because I wrote the sentence: "I score a lot of points in racquetball and
especially love playing it in the out of doors."

5. My friend Wendy Rojo has done my hair for nine years. She cannot believe I still have a strand of hair in my head due to the abuse we have given it over the years. "You have the strongest hair, Melissa. I don't know how it hasn't broken off at the root already." Whenever she says things like this I blush and feel so proud. I imagine it must be how some Olympian feels.

6. I sneak Chick-fil-A into movie theaters all the time, and they are either oblivious or used to me.

7. There is no place I would rather be than with my husband. I would hang out with him twenty-four hours a day if I didn't get on his nerves so much.

8. I find it hard to "find my place" a lot, and when that happens I am in the seventh grade all over again. Those feelings don't go away as you get older. You just get more adept at handling them.

9. I am awkward in crowds. I cannot make small talk, and I am funny at extremely inopportune times. Once I went with my husband to a big-wig Christmas party in Nashville with very lovely people who love Jesus and could afford hair extensions and expensive shoes. There, everyone made a stocking at the fancy-shmancy craft table. All the lovely, long-haired people wrote "Noel" or "Joy" or "Glad Tidings" on

their stocking. I wrote "Porn Star." I would like to personally apologize for my supreme awkwardness that night and just say that I felt really bad when, later that evening, everyone went and hung theirs on the tree while singing "Silent Night" and I had to hang mine beside the stocking with "Happy Birthday, Jesus" on it. I cried the whole way home, and no one ever invited me back.

10. I have zero fear of death. I heard the late Elizabeth Edwards say that once you have lost a child, death has no hold over you and it doesn't frighten you. She was right. Let's just say that when it's time...I've got people there. She also said, "If you know someone who has lost a child, and you're afraid to mention them because you think you might make them sad by reminding them that they died—you're not reminding them. They didn't forget they died. What you're reminding them of is that you remembered that they lived, and that is a great gift." She was right, and I need you all to know this.

11. I am Christian. Not the kind that protests at your funeral. Not the kind that protests your marriage. I am more the kind that laughs the loudest and jokes the saltiest. I forgive quickly and easily because that was what was done for me. I hate injustice and yet feel powerless

against it sometimes. So I pray, because God hates injustice, too. I want to tell you that I am a humble Christian, but nothing—*absolutely nothing*—could be further from the truth. I am working on this. I am also working on lying... because that last sentence I typed was a lie.

12. Both of my children are adopted. I am a *big fan* of adoption. *Huge!* I think everyone should do it. Absolutely everyone.

13. My children know they are adopted and have known since they were old enough to understand the part in Disney's *Tarzan* when the momma gorilla finds Tarzan and takes him home to live with her. We have hidden none of it from them. We honor their biological parents by using Mr. and Miss with their names and making them sound as wonderful as Iron Man or Wonder Woman. And why not? They are heroes, both in our home and in our hearts.

14. I smell everything. Listen to me: *everything.*

15. I have seen every episode of *Law & Order: SVU* ever aired, and I can tell you who did it about 3 percent of the time.

16. I do not know how I feel about certain issues until I ask my husband what he thinks. Or my mom. Or my friends. This should not be. It makes me feel weak and inept and not able to

form my own opinions and thoughts. And yet the thought of growing in this area seems overwhelming to me as I've been asking much longer than I've been deciding. You should know this is going to change very soon. I can no longer be worried about what it might cost me. I can only be concerned with the voice I might be lucky enough to find.

17. When I am nervous I talk really fast and really high.

18. I tried to make a top-five celebrity hot list, but I couldn't do it! I could only come up with one. Conan O'Brien. He's been my whole list forever. That's not to say that if I ever met Channing Tatum I wouldn't make sure there was no food in my teeth...

19. I started a long battle with depression my senior year of high school, and I excelled at it until I was in my thirties. Then I got freaking sick of it and decided to call it names and make it obey me. I became its boss instead of it becoming mine. I also talked to a therapist and learned all about myself and gave myself permission to cry when I wanted to cry and throw things when I wanted to throw things, as long as I cleaned up all the messes and no one else had to. I wish the story was better than that, but it isn't.

20. My earliest memory in my life was walking

down the hall late at night and finding my mom, alone on the couch, watching Johnny Carson. I crawled up beside her, watched him, and knew, even at a young age, that his was the best job in the world and he was the best at doing it. I cried the day he died.

21. I think about my weight every single solitary day of my life. Some days I am so unhappy with it that I don't want to leave the house. Other days I am unfettered and I dress up and *kill it*. If I took all the energy I give to my obsession with this imperfection, I would have immensely more energy to give to the things that actually matter. I am nothing if not a work in progress.

22. To the person who just scoffed and mumbled, "Then do something about it": If I find you, I'm going to punch you. To the person who just sighed and cried and uttered "me too": If I find you, I'm going to hold you.

23. I am a terrible friend. Horrible, really. I forget to respond to texts or emails, and don't even bother calling me because I'm not going to answer. I need you to talk about your problems 73 percent less than I talk about mine. And I am going to—whether you ask or not—tell you what to do with your hair. The good news in all of this? I tell people this up front, so the bar is low.

24. If I call you an idiot, a dummy, or a fool; joke

about your divorce; hide a stray cat in your car that you don't find until you get home; "forget" my wallet every time we go to dinner; or post obscene things to your Facebook timeline when you aren't looking, then this means I love you. I really, really love you so much it hurts.

25. I rarely finish anything.
26.

Chapter 2

Right after the Inhale.

Do away with all the HAPPY 40TH! party paraphernalia. Throw out all the black napkins and toss the FABULOUS AT 40 banner. Contact the party stores and the event planners. Believe me when I tell you, forty is not the issue. Don't bother throwing anyone a happy fortieth. They'll be fine. It's forty-one you need to focus on.

Forty-one is when you want to lie down in traffic.

Forty-one is when you want to dig a hole in your backyard and throw yourself in it.

Forty is a party, man. People are laughing, music is playing. It's a new chapter in your life, a new season. It's like you get a do-over for your obnoxious twenties. You read articles in *Cosmo* about how glamorous forty can be when you come into your identity and wisdom. And let's not forget about the whole "You hit your sexual peak" thing. *Hello!* Things are looking up. It's like you've been invited to some swanky middle-aged sorority where your pass to get in is that you must be over forty and have at least one funny story about how you pee when you sneeze.

No one remembers the pain of turning forty, because there's a party with friends all around you, and if they're good friends they brought a cake and lot of gifts. (Of course, if they're *real friends* they brought a gift and lots of cake.) My friends flash-mobbed me. That's right. David and I were eating at a small roadside crawfish restaurant that I love (don't judge me). David took forever to get ready—which was odd—and wound up getting us there just minutes before closing. We ordered our catfish right as they were turning off their neon OPEN light. We were sitting at one of their outside tables when car after car after car came driving in, honking, waving, screaming. I sat in disbelief as my friends rushed from their cars, set up tablecloths, and placed balloons on the tables beside me. One even picked up my plate and said, "Excuse me! We're having a party here," as she fluffed out a red and white checkered tablecloth and laid it on my table. A DJ set up in the corner while the gift table was created, and the lights of the restaurant turned back on as they prepared to churn out fried catfish and hushpuppies to everyone I loved.

It was a fun night and about as redneck as I am. We danced and laughed, and I let forty wash over me with hoopla and much fanfare. (My friends would also tell you that there is "false humility" and "crap humility," and that I am full of crap. They would tell you I reminded them of my fortieth birthday beginning the very first day of my thirty-ninth year. Do not believe them. They want attention.)

I had always imagined turning forty in a most somber way, quietly and alone, in a cabin somewhere, surrounded by weapons and icing in a can. But, hey, surround yourself with the right attitude and a lot of love, and you will have no choice but to celebrate!

Fast-forward to forty-one, and I'm thawing out a roast that's been in my freezer for seventeen months and picking up my own cookie cake in the mall.

Nobody calls you at forty-one.

No one throws you a party.

Some people give you a shout-out on Facebook, but all in all forty-one is your sign that what happened at forty was no joke, that it was real. It was the last birthday party you will ever have that is all just for fun and not planned with the intention of pitying you or because they are about to tell you that they're putting you in a home. After forty, you are on the downhill slide and going nowhere fast. Imagine it like one of those cartoons where the villain ties the woman to the train and it's headed off the side of the cliff and she's screaming. Only *you* are the woman and the villain refused to give you your reading glasses, so you aren't totally sure where you are or what all the signs are saying.

Yeah, that pretty much sums up what turning forty-one was like for me.

Also, my cookie cake said "Happy Birthday Mealissa." So...yeah...*it was awesome.*

On the first day of my forty-first year, I sat around a table that *I* had set, with a dinner *I* had made, a cake *I* had picked up, and kids *I* had just finished helping with math homework. David was celebrating the day I had arrived on earth by being willing to put the ice in the glasses. My parents walked in without even knocking because, per my mom, "knocking and ringing doorbells are for UPS drivers and Girl Scouts," so why on earth would they?

My dad saw the giant cookie cake and said, "Oh my word, is that today? And who's Mealissa?"

"Mealissa is me. And yes, it's today. Don't you even know when your own daughter's birthday is?"

My mom cut in. "Melissa, why don't you start eating *real* cake? Carrot is delicious."

"Of course I know when my own daughter's birthday is. December 1, 1973. Five fifty-five p.m. It's not what day you were born on I have a problem with—"

"It's what day it currently *is* that he has a problem with," my mom interrupted.

"So, what you're saying is you're stuck in 1973," I replied. "Well, that explains the mustache."

He laughed and hugged me. "Happy birthday, baby. Where are the kids? We brought them a little something."

(For those of you reading this book who do not yet have kids, grab a pen. Here is wisdom from your crazy, old aunt Mel: When you have kids, *they* get gifts on your birthday.)

I fixed my parents a plate even though they could "only stay a minute" and the six of us sat around the table and talked about our day. It was my favorite part of an otherwise awful Monday. I'm not going to lie: I had only gotten out of bed for the cookie cake. After dinner, my mom brought the cake over to the table and my kids sang to me. I froze that moment in my head.

———✦———

There sat David. This man who had met me when I was only nineteen and loved me still. Who had his first introduction to me on a school trip when I squeezed my smelly feet between the van seats he was sitting on right in front of me. The man whose first words to me were "Dang, your feet smell. Could you move them, please?" The man who remembers the first words I ever uttered to him: "I would, but I don't want you to fall in love with me." He had loved me well for the last twenty years of our lives together, and now here he sat, holding the son we'd never thought we'd have. His smile spread across his face. I was lucky to have found him then, and I was blessed to have him now.

Happy birthday to you . . .

David held on tightly to Rocco, who sang—off key—at the top of his lungs. His blond hair hung in his face, glued down by the sweat that all six-year-old boys create, even in December. Some of his front teeth were missing, making the "Happy Birthday" song one of the cutest things I had ever seen, with his tiny tongue filling up the gaps in his mouth. He looked like every dream I had ever had so many years before, when children had still not come. When I would close my eyes and imagine a son, they always looked like this boy sitting right here beside me. His eyes the color of mine and his temperament identical to his daddy's. David tried to hold him as he bounced and clapped and sang to me; I read his lips as he whispered for Rocco to "calm down."

Happy birthday to you . . .

Remi was singing to me, but her eyes were locked on the cake. I stared at her and smiled. The misspelling of my name finally registered on her face with a furrowed brow and look of shock. Even while continuing to sing, she looked up at me, appalled, not sure that I had seen the mistake, biding her time until she could rat out whoever had made it. She looked at me, then the cake. The cake, then me. The tiny gathering of freckles on her face and the blue in her eyes—she was stunning. She struck me as everything I ever hoped to be in my life. She may have been the very reason why this moment is so frozen in my mind. *This child.* This girl. This reward. This amazing creature of resilience and strength. In her pinky, she held more good than I held in my whole body. I wished for half a second that I could be eight again so I could choose her to hang with, but I knew the greater responsibility came not in knowing her but in raising her. Her eyes caught mine, and she must have decided that since I was staring at her, I had never noticed the misspelling in my name. To spare me the hurt (yeah, right), she ran her finger through the extra icing. Goodbye, extra *A*.

Happy birthday, dear Melissa...

My mom, pretending to sing, was focused on her Words with Friends game that had recently *dinged* us at dinner, indicating one of the ladies in her mahjong group had played the word *sudsy*, and now Mom was on the attack. Beside her was my dad. Furrowed brow, trying desperately to figure out what he could give me for my birthday that might look as if he put any thought into it, which he had not. Which didn't matter. My dad would take off his shirt and hand it to me if he thought I needed it. He was the most generous human I had ever met. Except for the handsome hunk at the other end of the table holding a rowdy six-year-old, I had never known a better man. In the middle of my birthday song he pulled out his wallet and looked through it. I watch him as he pulled out a hundred-dollar bill and folded it. My mother looked over, shook her head, and mouthed, "Uh-hhhh, no." He ignored her and slipped it under my plate.

Happy birthday to you.

My family was around me. They are loud and obnoxious and precious, and I am well loved. But I was also turning forty-one. The lit candles taunted me as if to say, *Make a wish, Mealissa. Not that it matters. Wishes quit working out for you around age fourteen when you wished that your boobs would stop growing.*

I looked at my candles, flickering.

I looked at my cake, giant.

I looked at my name, misspelled.

And I inhaled.

Stop.

Because the whole point of this book, the very reason it was ever written, the very reason I ever signed on the dotted line with an editor who tells me I start too many sentences with the word *And*, is all about what happened right after that inhale.

You might have thought this book was about cake. It isn't. I am so sorry to disappoint you, and if I could make it up to you by buying you an actual cake, I would, but

I'm out of town right now so I can't. This book is not so much about cake as it is about the night that I blew the candles out on my cake. My forty-first birthday cake.

Deep breath in...

That's life, you know. Everything starts right after the inhale. Don't let the symbolism of that escape you. Sit in that for a moment. You are who you are. Right now. Like it or hate it, this is you. Now, take a deep breath in.

Seriously, try it.

Right now.

Take a deep breath in and feel your lungs expand.

This, this moment right here. This is what we are talking about. We aren't talking about the inhale, we are talking about what comes right after it. Right after our lungs have expanded with possibilities or change or dreams or courage or promise.

Everything you are or need to be or hope to become— everything you want to try or face or confront or change—begins right after you inhale. You think you are filling your lungs with air, but you're not. You are filling your lungs with *what's next*.

It's you, getting another chance.

It's you, taking it all in.

It's you, letting it all go.

It's you, breathing in the new.

It's you, releasing the old.

It's you, sucking in every bit of a moment you don't soon want to forget.

It's me, at the table getting ready to make a wish and knowing that it comes right after the inhale.

That's when everything in my entire world changed forever. Right after the inhale.

———◄———

The room stopped, and everything in it was frozen but me. It seemed like forever as I looked around the table at the faces I loved, even though it was only seconds. My birthday moment was here. Every birthday was about this moment right here. The wish.

"Make a wish!"

"Make it count!"

"Don't tell your wish!"

"What did you wish for?"

The older we get, maybe we have less to wish for, less to hope for. But here I was, I was turning forty-one, and it was time to make a wish. As I closed my eyes and inhaled I said to myself:

I want to be brave.

The candles quit dancing and my kids clapped. They reached in to grab some cake with their hands like animals—because they have not secured one single table manner in their short lives—and I excused myself.

"You okay?" David asked.

I was fine. I just needed a minute. My mom slapped my kids' hands away and stood to get the plates and forks. I walked to my room and sat down on the edge of my bed. I took out my journal and a pen, and here is what I wrote in that journal on that very day:

———————

I want to be brave. God, please! I just want a moment of bravery. I'll worry about a lifetime later; just for now, give me a moment. Give me one minute, one second, when I don't second-guess or doubt. When I don't ask opinions, seek counsel, or "think on it." I want to say yes when everything tells me I should say no. I want to do what scares me. I want to live in a way that excites me. I don't want to miss out on "could" because I was too stuck doing "should." I am so tired of my life being determined by what someone said, what some mean girl thought, what some family member spoke, what some teacher—*whom I once saw wearing socks and Crocs, for God's sake*—etched on my frame. Who have I become that I have allowed their *no*s to be my answer? My daughter is watching me. She is watching me!

Melissa, wake up!

Today is your birthday. And the wish you made today, December 1, is to be brave.

This year, I will live brave. It will be new for me and I will be unsure of my footing probably most of the time, but I'm at least going to try. I don't think I could look my daughter in the face if I knew I had not at least tried. Happy birthday, Mealissa. Go eat cake and be brave.

———≡

I closed my journal. Walked into the kitchen and ripped off a piece of cookie cake with my bare hands. David looked at me like I was a nut. My mother rolled her eyes and my children clapped. They followed suit. We all grabbed a piece and shoved it in our mouths.

I did not worry about the calories.

I did not care about the carbs.

It was not fat-free or sugar-free. It was not dairy-free or gluten-free.

There was a very real chance it had 1,800 calories a slice and was made entirely of high fructose corn syrup. I didn't care. I didn't care that I had ordered it at a mall or picked it up from some kid with YOLO on his nametag. This was not "clean eating"; this was *dirrrrrty* eating, the dirtiest kind. And there, at my kitchen table, sat all the people I loved, and we were enjoying every flippin' second of it.

I wiped the frosting off my forty-one-year-old face as my mom looked at me and said, "That's nice, Melissa, real nice. I hope you know these children are watching you."

"Yes, I know they are. I hope they are." I was shocked to hear myself say that! I had never hoped that before. But yes, I hoped they were watching. I hoped that they watched me very closely in my forty-first year. The year I really started living.

Chapter 3

People Who Might Want to Think Twice before Asking Me for Money.

All I needed was some onion and a cantaloupe. That was it. Normally you'd think that would only take a second, but I'm not going to chop and peel two onions like some *loser*, so I was looking in the refrigerated section for the pre-chopped onions—*because I enjoy paying for my laziness*—when he approached me.

"I have been looking for you for years now."

I'm not on Tinder. Wait, am I?

"I heard you had moved back into town, and I was hoping I'd run into you years ago, and I'm so glad that I finally did!"

Still nothing...

"It's me." And then he pointed to his face, as if that should make all the difference, as if that would clear things up. But faces can change a lot in twenty-five years. God knows mine had. But I began to recall exactly who he was as he leaned in for a kiss on the cheek. I had endured thirteen long years with him. Kindergarten through twelfth grade he teased me, laughed at me, loved me, hated me; I never quite knew where I stood or what I might get from him. Our junior year he threw my purse in the cafeteria trash can and became breathless and red-faced as he watched me dig my way to the bottom looking for it. And for what? A hairbrush and two tampons, that's what. (In high school you'll scale a wall and face off with a pack of dogs for a discreetly hidden tampon.)

He had changed over the years. Once I realized who he was, I couldn't help but notice his face had softened, as had his approach. We exchanged the necessary things Southerners do (how's your family; where you workin' now; the obligatory list of people from our graduating class who have died), and then he said this:

I want you to know that I am so sorry about how I treated you in high school. Well, all throughout school, really. I was so insecure back then, and I think I took it out on you...a lot. I did some pretty terrible things to you, as I'm sure you can remember. And anyway, I've been hoping to run into you just so I could apologize and tell you how sorry I am and that I hoped you'd forgive me. That's not who I am anymore. So, I'm sorry.

If you noticed, I didn't write those words in quotes because I am not entirely sure of the exact words or pauses or phrasing and I don't want y'all holding me to anything. But also, the reason I don't remember them exactly is because...

1. It was foggy, people. I was losing consciousness. Everything was going blurry and foggy like that time I was asked to couples skate at a fifth-grade birthday party by my friend's dad because he felt sorry for me. But then they started playing "Secret Lovers" and he decided to go get more coffee. Yeah, it was like that.
2. I could not figure out what to do with my hands. I couldn't put them in my pockets because that would provide no external support were I to drop at any minute. I could either embrace him and hold that for an awkwardly long time, or I could rest them on some melons. I chose the melons. I chose—for some reason that I can only chalk up to my innumerable personality disorders—to support myself by placing my hands on some nearby melons. (Why I chose my boobs and not the table full of honeydews, I will never know.)

So, you'll forgive me if some of it is a blur.

We hugged goodbye, I grabbed a cantaloupe, and left. I forgot the onions and I forgot my senses and I almost forgot to pay, but apparently, I really *really* needed that cantaloupe. I got in my car and I drove.

I'm not sure how I drove or where I drove or even how long I drove—which should be a real comfort to those who were sharing a road with me that day—because as I do during most of life's emotionally exhausting moments, I blacked out. Oh, I'm sorry, when I mentioned that before, did you think I was kidding? Yeah, no. I tend to black out at things that cause me great duress (e.g., confrontations, important meetings, yard work). And if you don't believe me, you can ask my therapist. Emotional blackouts happen to certain types of people. Specifically, my types of people are people who color on the "emotional surplus" end of the spectrum. People who paint with an overly dramatic array of colors called:

- "Kill me now" khaki
- "Sweet Lord, blow your trumpet and return me to Glory" ginger
- "I'm not being dramatic, my flesh is literally melting" mint
- "If anyone says another word, Mommy is going to disappear for a year and a half" black

I cannot help it that absolutely everything I do has the emotional intensity of someone who is trying to book on

Orbitz. (By the way, booking on Orbitz? Bury me!) I just know that when I deal, I deal all the way. There is no in-between. To love you is to love you hard and forever. To be hurt by you is to be scarred here and there and every-where. I can forgive you, as I have learned how to do this. But I rarely forget. I used to think that was a necessity—*the forgetting*—but not anymore. I don't care how cute *Fifty First Dates* was; the forgetting would drive me bonkers. I don't want to live in a world where I forget over and over that the stove is hot. Or that you're a punk.

But to run into your high school nemesis while pick-ing out fresh produce? That right there's a jolt of reality. I would have called you a liar if you had tried to tell me that you ran into a nice, middle-aged man in a grocery store who kindly apologized, causing you to run out of the store like a six-year-old, get behind the wheel of your car, and drive until you found yourself four miles from your home sitting at a red metal table eating chicken wings. I would have laughed and called you a nut. But all I'm saying is: I'm not a big fan of chicken wings. You do the math.

And yet, you gotta give it up for the man who is big enough to come back and say he's sorry. There's something to be learned from those brave enough to ac-knowledge what very few ever really do, which is:

Who I was may in fact no longer be who I am.

But what about the folks who never come back?

Who never saw that what they did hurt you?

What about those who were never bothered enough to change?

Or who never changed enough to bother?

What about the ones we want to meet up with in a dark alley?

The ones we want to throat punch?

The ones we want to pants?

What do we do with these people?

Well, welcome to my Raise a Glass list. That's right! For every person listed here I will raise my glass of sweet tea, wave my hankie, and cry, "Bless them, Jesus!"

These are the people who, as my mother would say, have just "stuck in my craw." And although I can't track them down, *no matter how much money I once offered to pay an off-duty policeman*, I can write about them here. You know, just in case you can find them. Which I am certainly not asking you to do. But that would be hilarious. Anyway, *bless them, Jesus.*

So would you join me—I know you want to—in raising a glass:

To the 1984 graduate of Hudson High School who was given the duty of helping us fourth graders prepare for the Presidential Physical Fitness Test. (Because sending a blond-haired, blue-eyed senior boy over to weigh fourth grade girls is literally the best idea ever!) Thank you for weighing me, yelling my weight across the breezeway followed by the words, "Dang! This little girl better hope she doesn't have a heart attack." *Down the hatch!*

To Jason, who worked at the first job I ever had, slinging fried chicken at the Grandy's in Lufkin, Texas. He was tall and cute and funny and two years older than I. He offered to take me to my prom since no one had asked me, and I bought a dress that I had worshipped from afar for the last two years. A week before the prom he busted a gut when I told him the dress had arrived. "Oh God," he scoffed, "you thought I was serious?" *Salut!*

To Tiffany and Kelly, between whom I sat in college. If you are going to write notes about me, at the very least move them off your desk when I walk in. It's called decorum, ladies. I only know you did this because of the time I came in twenty-five minutes late and you had been debating where I could have been. I saw that you both must have clearly had my best interest at heart when you wrote "Dear God, I hope she's at Jenny Craig." For the record, you were both wrong. *Cheers!*

To the friends who left me when my marriage was in shambles and my tears were too much. Who shook your heads, waved your hankies, and gathered around the woman who tried to break up my marriage because "bless her heart, she must be so broken to do such a thing." You were wrong. I was so broken. I was the broken one. *L'chaim!*

And the most hurtful of all: To those of you who wouldn't even let me try. You wouldn't let me in the group or on the stage. You recognized my talent, but you hated my face. Don't you know I am not one without the other? You thought my face was too fat, my shoulders too slouched, and my dreams too big. And so here I sit, some years later with a face that didn't change all that much but a voice that just got louder. Because, eventually and over time, we heal from your words and from your smirks and from your disinterest. We heal from being left out, looked over, and laughed at. So, to the ones who still think the voice must match the body, that to sound good is to look good, and to the record producer who once told me, "You got a good voice, but unfortunately people just don't buy ugly"—thank you. My mom was right about you. *Bottoms up!*

So, what now?

What do we do with all that they did?

What do we do with the bullies, the mean girls, the side glances, and the cold stares?

We write a book and dedicate one whole chapter to them.

And we forgive them.

We do it every single day until we mean it.

We do it every single day until we can wish them well.

It doesn't mean we have to forget. Chances are we couldn't if we tried.

But we can forgive. Trust me, smaller people than us have forgiven bigger idiots than them.

Truth be told, every person I listed in this chapter was sent to teach me. They were all just part of the story. As Nora Ephron says, "Everything *is copy*," so we use them in our story and in our lyrics and in our monologues, we use them in our sermons and our cooking and our paintings. We use them when we want to reach way down and feel something for act 3, scene 4. We use them to make our parenting greater and our character stronger.

They were sent to serve you.

Sent to build you.

How did they do?

I'd say they did a great job. Look at you! Stronger, braver. You, my friend, are a force of nature. And they played a part in that.

But you *sure as heck* don't lend them any money or help them move.

Chapter 4
Cheerleaders: Part 1.

I suppose there are instances where the whole *if you can't beat 'em, join 'em* thing works; for instance, I hate shopping but if the carload of women I'm with will not bend to my ways and take in a matinee, I can do some damage in Sephora. And yes, if everyone wants Thai, I'll do Thai. And once, I had a colonic out of good old-fashioned peer pressure. But it doesn't always work! For example, I cannot pull myself out of my own swimming pool because of a complete lack of upper body strength, so my plan is to try out for that team Michael Phelps is on.

You see? You see how absurd that saying can be? I think I've proven my point.

And yet, from the age of nine until the ripe age of twenty-one I wanted nothing more than to be a cheerleader. I mean, I wanted zero else. I didn't need money or a fancy car, I wasn't after prom queen or class favorite. I just wanted to be a cheerleader. Like, *embarrassingly* bad. I know you're asking yourself: Why?

Alright, let's flesh this out.

Pleats. I know that sounds absurd but this was the eighties and early nineties, y'all! From Jordache and Z Cavaricci's, to Krystle Carrington and Jesse Spano, pleats were in, and *oh sweet Lord*, I loved the pleats. I wore pleated khaki britches or khaki shorts almost every day of my life. (Yeah, I just admitted that...and why not? I grew up before the Internet. I'm not ashamed of this. *Usually.* Wanna know something else? I still use a pick on my hair and I have an entire playlist dedicated entirely to New Edition.) But why pleats specifically? Because my mom—*who never met a dressing room she didn't like to invite herself into*—told me pleats were flattering for my body type and like a nut-in-a-hut I believed her. So, a cheerleading skirt? Could you not just die? An entire skirt made of nothing but pleats? I could not even fathom what that might mean for my ~~muscular chunky~~ muscular legs. So, you better believe that, after that—if it had pleats—I bought it.

My favorite pair of corduroy shorts.

My jeans.

I even had a nightgown with pleats in it.

I looked good in pleats and I was not going to let the world forget it. Besides, who doesn't want to look like a bank teller at 12? I don't mean to brag, but my ability to rock pleats and shoulder pads...well, it's probably why I'm so intimidating to women to this day.

Paula Abdul. Paula Abdul's "Straight Up" was my jam and when I saw the cheerleaders in my middle school run out to the floor and perform a routine to this song I was sure I had died and gone to VH1 heaven. I danced to this in my room every night. No one had ever seen such magic. (And when I say that "no one had ever seen such magic" I mean that no one, literally not one person, would come in my room and watch me dance.) But to think that I might could get lucky enough to perform it at school, on that old wooden gym floor, in front of some of the most critical and judgmental seventh graders I'd ever met? Heck yeah! I had to get out on that floor or die trying.

Flips. I will never be able to throw up without crying. I will never be able to listen to "True Colors" and not sing the alto line. And I will never, *ever,* be able to hurl my body into the air and it not kill me. But a cheerleader can! And I just could not comprehend this...*still can't.* They showed us astronauts being forced out of the earth's atmosphere on the TVs at school and I yawned. But show me a girl running full force and then, like a dummy, throwing her head toward astro turf? I was mesmerized.

The pyramid. Humans making a pyramid? The brilliance of it I cannot even explain. All I can tell you is there along the bottom were the girls that ruled the world. They knelt on their hands and knees, holding up life itself; and don't give me any of that, *"So Melissa, a doctor holding a human heart in his hand…"* fluff. You ask that doctor to get down on a cold gym floor and hold up Kayla, Kristy, and Marilyn and let's see how he does. These girls that served the bottom rung of that pyramid did it like a *beast.* Oh sure, most eyes went to the top and the adorable 5'2" petite balancing there—but not mine. I was certain I was ~~muscular chunky~~ muscular enough to be that base and shoulder the weight of the very people who totally ignored me in the halls. (Side note: Did you know that pyramids are now created *WHILE STANDING*? I cannot even talk about this. Someone dared to dream, you guys, *someone dared to dream.*)

And last, but not least: my cousin, Randi Jean. I adored her. She was six years older than me and I worshipped the wedges she walked on. I wanted to be her and wear my hair like her and be able to acquire a tan like her. One time when I walked in her room and overheard her saying to a friend on the phone, *"I cannot wait to graduate and get out of this hell hole,"* I cried myself to sleep that night at the thought of Randi *actually* going straight to hell for using such language. She was the coolest person I had ever met. Randi loved me very much and was always kind to me even though we had zero things in common. How were we different? Well, let's see…

When I was nine my mom was perming my hair once a month while Randi was mastering hot rollers.

She taught me how to lay out in the sun using nothing but baby oil; at the end of a particularly hot summer afternoon she had turned the color of perfect, golden toast while I had to be taken to the Emergency Room.

Her room was full of posters of Prince, who I was not allowed to listen to because my mom said he liked to *"fornicate in public, Melissa."*

She dated a guy who smoked! I could not fathom the depth of nonconformist she must have inside of her to date someone that I had not once seen without a cigarette in his mouth or sunglasses on his eyes.

She was so beautiful and popular and she had huge... dimples. For crying out loud, she was voted Prom Queen! Whereas everyone thought I was the Teacher's Aide and I eventually had to just start signing hall passes.

But our one common trait? She was no waif. She did not have stick-thin legs. In fact, with the exception that I bruised easily and was born with spider veins, our legs looked a lot alike. And yet hers were described as "muscular." When she put on her cheerleading outfit no one talked about weight or size. No! Instead they said things like, "Every good pyramid needs a solid base. Thank goodness for Randi!" I couldn't believe my ears! You could get away with murder in a cheerleading skirt. *(Edited to note: I believe there is a Lifetime movie about this very thing. I am not supporting nor endorsing it. But I did DVR it.)*

So yeah, I dressed up like a cheerleader every year for Halloween. That's right, every freakin' year, *what's it to ya?* I dressed up like a cheerleader when I was eight and I was still dressing up like one at seventeen. I'm not going to lie, dressing up like a cheerleader when you are eight has an entirely adorable quality to it. Dressing up like one at seventeen is just lazy because people assume you are actually a cheerleader and you just didn't want to spring for a different costume. Dressing up like one at seventeen *and you are NOT a cheerleader?* This is just weird. And sad. It is both weird and very sad. It's a bit less *Bring It On* and a bit more *Carrie.*

It's here in the story when people usually say, "Aaaah, Melissa, how cute! Why didn't you ever try out? You really should have tried out."

Oh, I did.

Thrice.

Do you know what "thrice" means? It means *three times*, it also means *extremely* or *very*. As in, "I very much tried out. I tried out an extreme amount of times. Three, in fact. I attempted a cartwheel thrice."

Let me tell you about the times I tried out for cheerleader. It won't take long because all three times began and ended the exact same way, so I can pretty much paraphrase them in a way you will understand and yet be made to feel like I am respecting your time:

I said, "I want to try out for cheerleader in front of my entire _____ school." (Insert middle / junior high / high.)

My parents said, "Nope."

I begged. I cried. I learned how to do the first part of a cartwheel behind their backs. But only the first part.

My parents still said "No."

I learned how to say "Ready! Okay!" in a really loud authoritative voice and my toe touches were sheer perfection as long as I always found myself in the vicinity of a trampoline.

Their answer remained the same.

"I don't understand! You know how much I want this, you know that I can do this! Aren't you tired of taking my Halloween costume back to the lady at the cleaners' who keeps commenting on how there's not much more seam she can let out? I am! Then let me try out and get a real cheerleading outfit! YOU KNOW HOW I LOOK IN PLEATS!"

My mother finally sat me down and said the words mothers today just don't say enough of: "Melissa Paige. You know I love you, and I love you too much to let you embarrass yourself."

I was stunned. I sat there quietly as she continued...

"Baby, I saw you trying to do a toe touch. And then I saw you keep an ice pack between your legs during dinner...."

I replied, "That's really not fair; I wasn't on a

trampoli.... You know what, doesn't matter. What about my cartwheels?"

"You broke my ottoman."

"Have you even seen me dance?"

"No, baby. But I've seen you try."

I remained stunned. "Well, what about my jumps?"

"Melissa, YOU CAN'T JUMP! I've never even seen you get off the ground!"

And then I was all, *"MOM! I GOT THIS!"*

Do you ever wonder what the first couple of episodes on *American Idol* would even be if parents all over the world were as brutally honest as my mom? What would they show us? I guess just a bunch of kids who could sing and play the guitar—because all the others were learning a trade or didn't skip school that day to embarrass themselves on national TV. I always wondered why no one was being honest with those who tried out and were painfully tone deaf.

DID NO ONE LOVE WILLIAM HUNG?

Why isn't someone being honest with them?

Where are their parents?

I'm sure I don't have to spell out the irony here. Just suffice it to say, their parent was probably in the kitchen loading the dishwasher muttering under their breath, "That child doesn't listen to a thing I say."

I don't really remember a lot about tryout number one. I think that's because of the head injury I suffered when I was running into a cartwheel/round-off but couldn't stop my momentum and hit the wall. There was a pad hanging on it for just such emergencies—so I didn't die. But I also didn't recover. I just know I did not make the squad and for the next three months people kept patting me on the back and telling me how hilarious I was. Also, I couldn't smell for about six weeks.

Tryout number two was especially awesome as it was my eighth-grade year just before I was headed into high school. Therefore, I had to try out in front of the entire high school. That's right! Back in the day you had to try out for cheerleader in front of the class you would be representing. So I, a chunky eighth-grader, with acne and size 10 flat feet, tried out in front of the entire high school I would soon be going into because that seemed like an *emotionally healthy* thing to do.

I didn't make it.

I ran out onto the gym floor to perform my routine and became so short of breath no one could hear a word I was saying. I had practiced my cheer so hard that I had never even thought to practice what it might sound like after a short jog. A runner, I am not.

Lastly, and in one of my more unforgettable high school memories, I worked myself up into a tizzy just before the gym door opened and I ran into the room screaming, "LET'S GO HORNETS! LET'S GO! C'MON! ON YOUR FEET!" only to realize that we were not, as we had been told, auditioning in front of faculty. Unbeknownst to me I had run right into a room with the cheerleading squad from Stephen F. Austin State University. With arms flailing, teeth showing, and a look of utter shock on my face, I tripped and broke a crown in front of the twenty-three members of a National-Division-winning university cheer team. One of their male cheerleaders offered to hold my crown for me while I performed.

Again, I didn't make it.

So yeah, I failed. Every time I tried, I failed. And every time—*all three horrifying times*—I went home in tears to my mother, who would wipe my tears, pull me close, put her hands on my chubby face and say, "Didn't I tell you this was going to happen? I told you! You never listen to me. You *alllllllllllways* know best, don't you? Now, sit down, baby . . . sit down and I'll make you some chicken strips."

I still love chicken strips to this day, and this story may be why I can rarely eat them without trying to do a toe touch.

Chapter 5

Seriously, How Much Do I Look Like Elisabeth Shue in This Picture?

Ugh! I hate telling this story. I didn't even want to tell it, but my editor is making me. Stupid editor. I hate her, with her "tell your best story and live your best life" mumbo-jumbo and perfect hair. (Also, my editor is not Oprah.)

To tell this story, I have to go back in my mind to 1987, and, honest to God, who wants to travel back to 1987? I mean seriously, of all the years? It wasn't like super cool 1985 with its *We Are the World* album, or even 1989 with the fall of the Berlin Wall and the release of "I'll Be Loving You Forever" by NKOTB. This was 1987. This was the year of AIDS, Jim and Tammy Faye

Bakker, and the creation of Prozac. I know, right? I'm depressed just writing those sentences. (Thanks for nothing, Prozac.)

Now imagine being thirteen. Now imagine it with a perm.

Yeah, you've just imagined me.

Oh, seventh grade. With your awkwardness and complete lack of self-awareness. In sixth grade we were crossing monkey bars and drinking orange Slice. By seventh grade we were trying desperately not to fart as Rosa held our feet down for sit-ups and orange Slice caused a crushing case of acne. You were not a great friend to me, seventh grade. I mean, you aren't grade school anymore and you aren't quite high school. You are like the Jan Brady of school grades. And we were so desperate to figure out who we were because once we figured it out, we would have only our eighth-grade year to perfect that person and make any necessary changes before we were then thrust into high school, where what we were when we walked down those halls the very first time would stay with us forever. So, seventh grade feels a lot like true crime TV where they've secretly recorded some hooligans trying to "get their story straight."

I remember the night before my seventh-grade year. I could barely sleep, I was so excited. I lay in bed staring at my closet where my clothes hung perfectly pressed for the day ahead. A three-button collared pullover in canary yellow, a blue denim miniskirt, white turn-down ankle socks, and white Keds. Keds were in. I would be in and I was ready.

Fast-forward to the middle of the school year and you'd find me dreading the bell that rang signaling lunch. Everyone would make their way out of the classrooms and into the halls, grabbing their lunches from their lockers, and on to the cafeteria, where they would meet up with their friends. But where do you go if you have no friends? You eat in bathroom stall number 3 with your feet on the toilet seat, so no one will know that you're in there. And that's exactly what I did. Every day. For almost a year. I ate alone in bathroom stall number 3.

I should point out I was not a leper. At least I don't think I was. You might want to ask someone who remembers me from back then; they may disagree. I was in seventh grade with the same kids I was in kindergarten with. I was in kindergarten with the same kids I graduated from high school with. My school was—and is—a throwback. There is no changing to schools across town, no east campus/west campus. You leave the same bubble you arrived in. So the problem wasn't that I didn't know them. It wasn't that I didn't like them. It was that I didn't know me. I wasn't a big fan of me, either. When we become adults, we use the phrase *fit in* casually, as if we are talking about sliding into a pair of jeans. We aren't. We are children, and when we don't fit in anywhere, it is a personal message that we may not fit in anywhere, ever. And whereas an adult can buy a different pair of jeans or lie flat across the bed to zip them up, we children can't outrun our skin and our weight and the embarrassing fact that we wear a larger size shoe than the principal—the forty-eight-year-old male principal.

And this was my world... in stall number 3.

I sat still as teachers came in and touched up their makeup and complained about their husbands.

I sat still as girls came in crying about the boy they liked or the grade they got.

I sat still and listened as sleepovers were planned and secrets were shared.

No one knew I was there. No one ever knew I was there. And although I don't remember many moments when I was literally alone during that lunch period, it was without a doubt the loneliest feeling in the world.

Man, it's hard being thirteen.

I eventually told my mom where I was spending my lunch periods, and she took it about as well as I would take it if my daughter told me she was eating alone, curled up on a toilet. She cried. I remember seeing her cry and wondering why she was crying. Was she surprised by this? Surely not. She had noticed me not going to birthday parties, right? She was aware there had been no Friday night sleepovers, no Saturday meet-ups at the mall. What was she so upset about?

I know now.

None of us wants our child to be left out. Ask any parent worth their weight and they will tell you that even if it means they have to sit very still and never make a peep, even if it means lifting their legs up so no one will notice the same shoes in stall number 3 every day, even if it means waiting until the coast is clear to pull their sandwich out of its bag, they would do it. Without hesitation. Without question. They would do it for their child every single time. If they could. But my mom couldn't. Seventh grade was mine: mine to handle, mine to figure out. Little did I know seventh grade was preparing me for the rest of my life. Not the bathroom stall part. That was just pathetic. No, this part of the story, right here...

She asked me if I was being myself. How could they not like me if I was being myself? (There's the parental comment heard 'round the globe: *How could they not like you? You're wonderful!*)

"I don't know if I'm being myself, Mom. How am I supposed to know that? I'm too busy trying to be someone that they like to know if I'm truly being myself."

Well, are you being funny? You are so funny, Melissa. People tell you that all the time, and they are right, you can make people laugh and that's why I cannot figure out why you aren't making good friends, you aren't being off-color are you, don't go for the easy laugh, Melissa, really successful comedians never go for the easy laugh and I certainly don't want you doing that in the seventh grade, it's inappropriate and besides, I don't even know where you would hear that kind of language, we don't talk like that at home, Melissa, where are you hearing such garbage?

Are you being kind? No one likes a mean person, and remember that poster I bought for your room that says "to have a friend is to be a friend" and that is so true, you need to remember that, if you want to have a friend then you should be a friend first, I think you have this problem because you are an only child and only children don't know how to talk to people as well as some kids and that's not your fault, that's our doing, but that doesn't mean you have to be a snob, I didn't raise you to be a snob, I'm not like that and your daddy's not like that and let me tell you something, Missy, you aren't going to be, either. Are you being a friend to others? Look for someone else who is lonely, Melissa. Someone else who might need a friend and then you can be their friend and then y'all can be friends with other lonely people and all sit together at lunch and why don't you invite them over for a sleepover, does a sleepover sound fun, I'll fix burgers, how about this Friday night? Are you being smart? Don't try to hide how smart you are, you are *really smart*, Melissa. That might be intimidating to some people, Melissa, but not the people that really matter because they will accept you, Melissa, and if it intimidates the boys well then they weren't good enough for you anyway, right, they shouldn't be intimidated because you can spell, Melissa, you always were such a good speller, show us, spell something for us right now, Melissa, spell something!

———◄≡

I could not stop the onslaught of questions my mother was throwing at me, and I most certainly didn't have answers to any of them. Not that she was pausing long enough for me to give one. (But hey! Here's a thing I know: *Is my hair permed?* I knew the answer to that. Hey, Mom, maybe you should've asked me about the body wave I didn't ask you to give me. Let's start there.) I knew her heart was in the right place. I saw that she was hurting for me, and I knew that if she could have gone to school and made friends for me she would have, but she couldn't. So she permed my hair. That's the thing about my mom that stands true to this day:

1. If she could replace my hurting with her hurting, she would.
2. She believes a perm really can change your life.

I appreciated her effort and promised to try. I wasn't sure what that would look like, but I was willing to come out of the bathroom and try one more time.

One particular afternoon, I was walking to my last class of the day when the teacher, who stood outside her door every day, stopped me before going in.

"Melissa, I hear you can sing."

How does one hear something like that? Are the teachers discussing various tween talents in the teachers' lounge? Because I knew they weren't talking about it in the bathroom. Ha! You get it? Because I was in there. Anyway...

"No, I can't." (Be yourself, Melissa.) "Yes, I can."

"Well, I would love to hear you sometime."

And I would love to let you hear me, because what could possibly be worse than eating on a toilet? Oh yes, I know, standing in front of a classroom of my peers in a miniskirt that is too tight with a face that Clearasil cannot fix and belting out a number. Yes! That sounds like a marvelous plan that I cannot wait to kill myself over. (Are you being kind, Melissa?) "Yes, ma'am, that sounds good."

"Great. Take your seat."

We were twenty minutes away from the bell ringing when she walked to the front of the class and said we had a special treat that day. I didn't know about anyone else, but I could always use a special treat.

"Students, did you know that Melissa can sing?"

And then I died. Well, not literally, because you're reading this book right now and trust me, I wrote it. But inside my thirteen-year-old self, I closed my eyes, held my breath, and begged for God to take me.

Everyone looked at me. No one laughed. Or clapped. Or said, "I knew it! I knew she must have a great talent! After all, her mom told us she was wonderful." Nope. They didn't say one word.

"Melissa, why don't you come—"

(Oh God, no. Please, no.)

"up here and—"

(This is not happening. Surely this is not happening...)

"sing something for us."

Everything in my world completely stopped, and I

could hear my thoughts so clearly you would've thought I was speaking them out loud. I sat perfectly still. She would not relent. And Lord knows I couldn't run. So I sat and thought. Not about how to fake an illness and not about how to escape. I thought about the song I would sing. And then I stood up from my desk and walked toward the front of the room.

Now, this is the part of the movie where everything turns into slow motion. My walk is in slow motion. The kids glaring at me like a tiny room full of serial killers is in slow motion. My teacher clapping before I had even made it up to the front is in slow motion. Everything is in slo-mo except my words, which are silently rushing out of my head: *Just be yourself. Look at her smiling and clapping and probably wanting you to sing something like "Amazing Grace," but "Amazing Grace" won't have 'em talking tomorrow. So, if you are going to entertain them, Melissa, entertain them. This is the only shot you've got to get out from behind door number 3. You can't help it if they hate you, if they look at you weird or avoid you like the plague. But you can do everything in your power to make them sit up in their seats and have a good time. That is the one thing you and I both know you can do.*

I really wish the "haters gonna hate" saying had been around at that time, as I'm sure I would've said that to pump myself up, but it wasn't, so I did the best I could with what the eighties gave us.

With that pep talk I walked to the front of the room

and sang—nay, belted out—"Keep Your Hands to Yourself" by Georgia Satellites. What do you mean you don't know it?

"I got a little change in my pocket goin' jing-a-ling-a-ling..."

Doesn't that ring-a-ling-a-ling any bells? (I'd quote the rest of the song here for you, but I'm not paying that kind of money.)

By the time I reached the second line the room was clapping. (Self-discovery alert: Clapping encourages me.) Those poor kids never stood a chance. The more they clapped, the louder I got. The louder I got, the more confident I got. And the more confident I got, the more fun they had. By the time the bell rang, everyone was clapping and laughing and there stood my teacher with her jaw dropped and her eyes wide. But I wouldn't apologize. I had been myself. Nothing I did in that moment was contrary to who I was.

I loved to sing.

I loved to entertain.

I loved seeing people laugh and knowing that I was responsible for it. That I had created a moment where seventh grade didn't matter, the terrible haircut our mom gave us didn't matter, and what we wore and how well we wore it wasn't a determining factor of just enjoying the moment. I looked around and saw that for a couple of minutes I leveled the playing field for everyone in that seventh-grade class. No one is an athlete or a mathlete in a room full of laughter. Everybody is just laughing. And I realized that's what humor can do. It can be those black kneepads Kerri Walsh Jennings wears during a game. Eventually things are going to get rough. You won't always land on your feet, and sometimes you'll have to get low and throw yourself at the mercy of the game. Best have something that softens the fall. Also, best to rock a bikini like Kerri Walsh Jennings, if at all possible.

So, in conclusion, here are the real takeaways from this chapter: Laughter levels the playing field, looking like an Olympian in a bikini never hurt anybody, and seventh grade blows chunks.

Truth is, it was much easier to write this chapter than to have lived it. Just like it's easier to see what's behind you from a rearview mirror of a car moving straight ahead. But life isn't like that. Life doesn't give you drone footage, with a view up above the trees and the weeds, soaring above the unhappy home life or the not fitting in. The best we can do with all that *was* is to speak to it on behalf of all that now *is*. So, to that:

Dear Thirteen-Year-Old Melissa,

I feel like I know you well enough to be perfectly frank with you. You are a hot mess. You know this.

I am not telling you anything you don't know. You look at other girls your age and wonder how they have it together at thirteen. I know! I don't get that, either. But some people just come out of the womb knowing how to match clothes and fix hair. You are not this person. And that matters right now; it matters a lot. And guess when it will stop mattering? No clue. I'm in my forties and have yet to see the day that looking put together and well-polished doesn't matter. (Also, good news for you, I have yet to find the day that we do, in fact, look put together. So, you have that to look forward to . . . my apologies.)

I know that right now your legs are longer than everyone else's and not in a really awesome Elle Macpherson kind of way. I know you shop in the women's section. And I know your mom thought if she permed your hair you would look just like the girl in *Karate Kid*, and I know it was devastating to learn, only after it was done, that you looked more like the evil sensei. Trust me, I know all of these things. I also know that anytime someone writes a letter to their younger self, it is so they can reassure them that "yes, things will turn around . . . you will grow into your legs . . . and everything will be better than you ever thought."

Yeah . . . *no*. Not so much.

You see, Melissa, our story is different. (I mean,

we do eventually grow into our legs, but not the way you're hoping. I'll leave it at that and let you be surprised.) But we grow into something else. And it really all started the day you walked out of stall number 3 and into your English class with Mrs. Price. Because, Melissa, on that day in 1987, you discovered a part of yourself that most people don't discover until much, *much* later, if it is ever truly discovered at all. You discovered what you were good at. And you discovered that what you were good at just happened to be what you loved. And that, my little friend, is a rare find.

Your journey from the toilet to today will not be an easy one. No one walks up to you in high school and says, "Melissa, you're so lucky that you discovered music and writing and comedy at an early age. What a beautifully crafted life you have at only sixteen." There's much less of that and much more of them looking at you like you are a really funny alien. Let 'em. It won't kill you. In fact, people will look at you funny for the majority of your life. They'll say you're too much or too loud, too confident or not confident enough. They will label you a diva, a disaster, and a dumb blonde. You will never be able to do math. And your approach when speaking to anyone who cannot speak English is to talk twelve decibels louder in hopes that will help. You are going to be terribly lazy and terribly creative, and usually those people end up on drugs, so careful there.

But, Melissa, you are one of a kind. A force to be reckoned with. You don't see that now, but you will. Because one day you will have children of your own and you will see in them the wonder that our mother saw in us. And you will hear yourself say to them, "Who wouldn't like you? You're wonderful!" And that will instantly bring you back to 1987 and you'll laugh. Because she was right. Who couldn't love us? We stand up in front of people and sing Georgia Satellites. And when we do, we realize that everything we will need was always in us, always right here...behind door number 3. Don't ever fear eating an occasional lunch behind that door. Fear living behind it.

Love,
Me or Us or whatever

P.S. That day, after the bell rang, you walked to your locker with three girls you'd known since kinder-garten but had never really talked to. Mom would tell you it was because being true to who you are is about the little choices you are faced with every day, and in that split second in the classroom, Melissa, you decided to just be yourself and it was enough. It was *so* enough. I guess Mom was right...*oh screw it:*

I know Mom was right. You ended up making a lot of memories with those girls, and most of them were made around the lunch table. Which only goes to show you that the hits of the eighties—when used the right way—can bring us all together.

Chapter 6
Cheerleaders: Part 2.

Guess what other place has cheerleaders? College! *Sweet-mercifulfather,* they are in college, too.

Only these guys and girls are hard-core! I once saw a guy throw a girl up in the air, lean down, tie his shoe, and still have enough time to catch her. And I kid you not, there was the time I saw one girl jump off another one's shoulders, flip in the air, and land flat on her face. She jumped right up and yelled, "That's how we do it! *Go Lions!*"

Whaaaat?

Y'all, I watched them like I was watching mating season on the Serengeti; I couldn't take my eyes off them.

They all had so much rhythm. And they could dance! (Not like the time I danced in my room to "Twist and Shout" and then lived on crutches for three months. *They* could really dance.)

Let me tell you, as fun as it is to sit by a cheerleader in English lit your sophomore year of high school, it's even more fun to share a hall with them in the dorms. Aaaaah, yes, how *superduperawesome* it is to share that one big adjoining bathroom. Let me tell you: Self-harm happens when you see a cheerleader step out of the shower with one regular-sized towel from JC Penney draped neatly around her and tucked in right under her arm...and you know the only towel that you can tuck in like that is the beach towel your dad bought in Panama City that says I CAN'T. I HAVE CRABS. on it. Good times.

So, what made me think fixing one of them up with one of my best friends would be a smart plan?

I liked David. David was a good guy. A bit of a womanizer and a bit arrogant and clueless about fashion—but I liked him. He made me laugh and he always paid. I don't know about you, but that's all I was looking for my freshman year of college: a good, free time. We had been friends since the beginning of school and hanging out with him was one of my favorite things, but let's call a spade a spade: The guy was looking for a good time! And boy, did I have the girl for him...

He was cute, she was cute.

He liked chasing women, she liked being chased.

He cared about looks and not much else, and she could put her legs over her head. What could possibly go wrong?

I fixed them up, and in no time at all he was waving bye to me as they sped off the school campus and she enjoyed my free meal.

I saw less and less of David as the months wore on, and—I cannot tell a lie—it was getting old. I missed him. I missed late-night movies and patty melts at IHOP. I missed stalking our least favorite professors. I even missed listening to his horrible jokes. I missed pretending to care about the Dallas Cowboys and how he pretended to listen to me talk about *Melrose Place*. I was so thankful for the weekends she left to visit her family out of town. On those weekends, I knew David was mine, all mine...and I could expect a weekend of belly laughs and free movie popcorn! We had a great time and the best part? He never mentioned her.

Until this one time...

Our last class ended and it was time for the weekend. Sha-Na-Na (this was not her legal name so much as it was the name I gave to her behind her back...where she couldn't hear me...and her cheerleader friends couldn't hear me...and they couldn't double-backflip-with-a-full-extended-somersault over me) was headed to her parents' house, and David and I had made plans to grab dinner and do some Christmas shopping at the Galleria.

Side note: Doesn't this all sound very Sandra Bullock/Hugh

Grant rom-com? I know, right? And if I'm being honest, my life up to this point had not consisted of a great deal of Sandra Bullock/Hugh Grant moments as much as it had consisted of me going on about three dates total. One of which was super special because the guy yawned all night while saying things like, "This will teach me to slice up a deer on the same day I gotta take a girl out."

So yeah, I was excited. I ran back to my dorm to put on comfortable shoes (because even at nineteen, heel spurs!), and I flung my door open to see what looked like the entire Southeastern Conference of cheerleaders all lined up in my room, Sha-Na-Na sitting right in the dead center of them.

Any normal person would have questioned their reason for trespassing. And yet, immediately I thought, *Have they come to ask me to join the squad? Should I have limbered up for this moment? If I were to drop into a full split right here, right now, how far down would I actually go?*

"I thought you were headed out of town for the weekend?" I asked.

"I changed my mind. Where are you going?" she asked. Although I had seen enough *Melrose* to know, this was not a legitimate question as much as it was a question she already knew the answer to.

"I was going to hang out with David, but since you're here, I'm sure he'll want to..."

"Oh no. You go ahead. You can go out with him. I hope you both have a great time. I think it's sweet that he does something with you—you're like a little brother to him. And I know that's why he loves hanging out with you so much, ya know? Because he's bored to death...so yeah, go ahead."

"Um, thank you?"

"But do me a favor, won't you? Ask him about me."

"What are you talking about?"

"I. Want. To. Know. What. He's. Thinking. I mean, where is this relationship going? I just find it so super weird that he spends time with you whenever I'm gone...but there's really not a lot else to do around here...so I guess I get that. But is he serious about me? I want to know. Mmmkay?"

"How am I supposed to do that?"

And then—because it was all we had, kids—she pulled out the most amazing piece of recording technology known to man: a Sony Walkman. (Google it.) She unzipped my purse. She placed the tape recorder inside, just below the surface of the zipper, pressed Record, and zipped my purse up only halfway.

"Just like that. Get him to talk about me and let me hear what he says."

I'm embarrassed to admit this next part. But I've come too far to lie now.

"*Okay!*" I said.

God, I loved a good caper.

"He'll talk to you. Talking to you is just like talking to one of the guys, you know?" she said as she brushed past me. "So, get the scoop and we'll meet back here after. Okeee?"

And with that, they were gone. The cheerleaders had come into my world, backflipped all over it, and left. My room reeked of Aussie Sprunch Spray and Elizabeth Arden's Red Door. But the squad had asked for my help. Mine! Finally, they needed me to be the base of their pyramid (scheme), and I obliged.

I obliged because I had always just wanted to be a part.

I obliged because what if, by some strange chance, one of them broke her foot later in the evening and they were like, "Well, we're headed over to Melissa's later anyway, why don't we just ask her?"

I obliged because her words had stung: "Little brother"? "Bored to death"? "One of the guys"?

And I obliged because someone had told me about that stupid "If you can't beat 'em, join 'em" crap—and like an idiot, I believed them.

I made sure the Record button was on and made my way to his car.

It's time I tell you that David, for being an extremely smart guy, was frighteningly easy to manipulate. Heaven help us all if the media ever gets hold of him; they'll have his Social Security number before they know they need it. I had been in the car with David all of ten minutes when I asked him how things were going with Sha-Na-Na, and he showed every card in his deck.

1. Her car was awesome.
2. She let him drive her car.
3. Had I seen her car?
4. Do you know how fast that car goes?
5. She's hot.
6. And her car ain't bad, either.

Okay, well, these Sony Walkmans have erase capabilities, right? We can just erase, erase, erase, and no one has to be the wiser. Yep, this was all going to be great. I had this all under control.

David and I loved Checkers. (Have you ever been to Checkers? Don't look directly at their food; just put it in your mouth and you will be so happy.) But he wasn't driving to Checkers. I knew it! He had discovered the tape and was going to murder me. There would be no free cheese sticks tonight!

Suddenly he pulled into the parking lot of the nicest, newest Italian restaurant in Dallas. You've probably never heard of it because it's pricey: Macaroni Grill. They had paper tablecloths! Wait, wouldn't that be paper table covers? Doesn't matter. What matters is—I was getting to go there! And it wasn't even for some wedding rehearsal dinner where I had to be another bridesmaid! (Man, except for the parts where David made a complete fool of himself while unknowingly being recorded by his best friend, this was shaping up to be a great night!)

I set my purse on the table to make sure it picked up

every word; I would work Sha-Na-Na back into the conversation if it killed me. Before long our bread was in front of us, and we were moments away from ordering something called *farfalle* when David's face grew white. (And this is really saying something, you guys, because he is one severely white man as it is; I once heard his mom ask him if he had "the virus.") At first I thought he was getting sick, which would have been so very sad for me, because I love Italian.

But then he spoke. "Melissa, did you know you are my best friend?"

"I figured. Oh my God, this bread is so goooooooooo-oood."

"I just...sometimes...well, here's the...what I'm trying to say..."

"Are you gonna eat that bread?"

"No. You can have it. Listen. I want you to know that if anything exciting in my day happens, you're the first person I want to tell. If anything terrible happens, I only think about telling you..."

"So if I reach over to get your piece of bread you're not going to—"

Wait. What?

"You fixed me up with her and we have a lot of fun and she's actually pretty cool, but the thing is, when I'm with her all I think about is you. And..."

"..."

"So, I just wanted to tell you that I'd like tonight to be

our first official date. If you're cool with that. Because I pretty much think you're the most incredible person I've ever met and I thought I ought to snatch you up before someone else does."

" . . ."

"You're not saying anything."

"Would you excuse me? I have to go to my purse. I mean, I have to go to the bathroom and also my purse. *My purse and I have to go to the bathroom!*"

I left. I stopped mere feet away from the table, gathered my thoughts, and returned. "And also this piece of bread that I need to eat bread for to eat." I grabbed what was left of the loaf, ran into a chair, and ran away.

I was not Sandra Bullock in that moment.

I walked into the bathroom, took the Walkman out of my purse, and put my mouth up to it. "I am not sure . . . so here's the deal. . . . I have to go now . . . I'm cutting this off now." And I did. I cut it off. And then I did what every fluffy white girl who never got asked to prom does: I began to dance. Not where anyone could see, short enough to be happy, long enough to be winded. Then I walked back to the table and ate about four pounds of chicken parm.

Oh, and also, I did not erase that tape.

No one had ever spoken to me like that before. Oh sure, the boys loved me when they needed someone to make them laugh or share a pizza with. They loved me when it came to toilet-papering someone's house or setting off fire alarms (that only happened one time). They called me when they needed someone to tell a dirty joke to or help them steal a dog (again, only once). But to date? They never wanted to date me. I had assumed I was undateable. I had wanted to be a dateable female about as much as I had wanted to be a cheering one. But there were just certain circles you don't make it into and those two were mine.

Dating and cheering. They were my kryptonite.

And then David.

I made David stutter. I made his already pasty white skin turn even whiter. I made him laugh nervously and open car doors for me. I made him not only want to hold my hand, I made him nervous enough *to ask* if he could! That's pretty much the only other thing I remember about our date. On our way back to the dorms he asked if he could hold my hand and I said yes. Hugh Grant had nothing on David.

That would have been the end of the evening.

Except it most certainly was not.

I arrived back at my dorm and I was three feet taller, ten pounds lighter, and heel-spur-free! I'm kidding. I was still a hot mess. But I was a mess with a boyfriend!

I ran up the stairs to my room, threw open my door, and there they all sat, looking like they had just walked off the set of *The Positively True Adventures of the Alleged Texas Cheerleader-Murdering Mom.* (Not that I ever saw that a few times.) Except that this time, if your eyes followed the line of cheerleader uniforms lined up against my wall, it would end on my girlfriend Kasey. Kasey was a bit—*how do I put this?*—fluffy like me. Her brown eyes were as big as frying pans and she shrugged her shoulders at me as if to say, "Was I supposed to lock your door?" or "Do I smell chicken parm on your breath?" I'm not sure which, and it didn't matter.

"Put it in," Sha-Na-Na said.

"Well, hello to you, too, ladies. How was your evening? Did y'all sit here all night? Please tell me that you didn't."

"Put. It. In."

"That's what she said! *Amiright?*"

"Melissa. We are done waiting. Put in the tape."

"Okay, but before I do, Kasey, could I see you outside in the hall for a moment?"

Kasey slid out from where she was sitting and followed me into the hall.

"Do I smell chicken parm on your breath?" she asked.

"Kasey, listen to me."

"Mel, they are really wanting to listen to this tape."

"Well, there is a little problem. Not even a little problem, just a skoosh of a problem, really."

"You better let them hear it or they are going to kill us with their hair, Melissa. Seriously! They're going to suffocate us with their hair or their perfume..."

"He said he's in love with me."

"Because both of those things are so strong I could barely even...whhhhaaaaaaaatttt did you just say?"

"HetookmeouttoeatandthistimeitwasnottoCheckers-
hetookmetoarealplaceandhetoldmethathewantedtobe-
morethanfriendsandhethoughthehadfalleninlovewithme-
andwantedtonighttobeourfirstofficialdateandthenheheld-
myhand."

"So, you *did* have chicken parmesan!"

And then, in a scene that would have made Mindy
Kaling so happy, we hugged each other's necks and
jumped up and down for like ten seconds. Because any
more than that is obnoxious. Plus, boobs.

"You are going to play them the tape!"

"I'm so confused. I mean it would totally embarrass
David. Plus, he talked about her and it wasn't pretty."
That's when we stopped and really thought about what
was at stake here. Listen, America. It wasn't just about
David. If it had only been about him, I might have done
things so very differently. I just want you to know that
before you read any further.

Kasey looked me in the eye, grabbed the collar on my
shirt, and said these words: "Melissa. Tonight is for every
little girl who has been told 'you're just big-boned' or
'you've got a great personality.' It's for the time you accidentally walked into the teachers' lounge at school and
someone asked if you were the new substitute teacher
when you were actually just a fifth grader. Do you understand me?"

Kasey was right! This was for them! And who was I
to stop this thing from happening? This was my Joan of

Arc moment. No, not Joan of Arc. I don't know a lot about what she did. But it was definitely my Goonies moment and just like a tiny, adorable Sean Astin, I was standing there saying, "Because it's their time. Their time! Up there! Down here, it's our time. It's our time down here." (See? You aren't as mad at me now, are you, because I made you think about Josh Brolin and when we do that, everyone wins. Except David. And definitely not Sha-Na-Na. But I digress...)

"C'mon. Let's do this!" Kasey pulled me toward the door. But before we walked back in, she turned to me, and with all the drama we could create (and it was a healthy amount) she whispered, "We've changed the world tonight, Mel. We are about to bring down a cheer-leading squad. Us! Mainly you. But also, me. Don't ever let them tell us carbs aren't our friends."

And we went in.

And we played the tape.

And when they left my room, they filed out in the most glorious display of #squadgoals that I had ever seen; they seemed almost to strut out but in a perfect line and all of them somehow knew to start with the right foot. It was really a thing of beauty. They walked with such force and precision that I believe somewhere in Houston, Texas, a tiny, baby Beyoncé first formed the words, "Come on, girls, let's get in formation."

They didn't turn to look at me and they didn't say a word. I thought I heard one of them whimper a bit, but

Kasey said that was because she had seen her eating only a packet of ketchup in the cafeteria for lunch.

Sha-Na-Na was out of my life forever. But not David's, not yet.

I could hear her screaming at him over the phone from down the hall. I bet he was wishing we were together right now and I was making him laugh and feel all those butterflies in his stomach, and I bet he was dreaming about wanting to touch my hair and whisper in my ear. That's how I imagined it at least.

And yet that was not the look in his eye when I walked downstairs to meet him about thirty minutes later.

"Bring the tape" was all he said.

He placed the tape behind the left front tire of his car and got in behind the wheel.

"You know, I'm not going to be a pushy girlfriend, but you always open the door for me, and yet you didn't open it just now, so I'm a little disa—"

"Get in the car," he said as he stared at me with a look that shut me down and shut me up. And from inside the car I watched him slowly back over the tape and then roll over it and back over and then roll over and back over and then roll over "our tape." Our first mixtape, so to speak.

He backed his car slowly out of the campus parking lot and, without saying one word, drove several blocks away from the school. Then we made out for a really loooooong time!

This was, hands down, the hottest caper I had ever been involved in.

Do I regret not having that tape? Yes. Do I regret taping him? No. We have now been married twenty-three years, and seventeen of those have been awesome! We still make out. Last I heard, She-Na-Na had put on quite a bit of weight and acquired tennis elbow.

And that, my friends, is how the good girl *does indeed* get the guy.

The Truth about My First Date.

Chapter 7

The first story I ever wrote, I wrote in college. It wasn't a term paper or a thesis; it wasn't only a paragraph or two—it was a straight legit story. Except it wasn't totally legit in that I lied in it. Please allow me a moment to correct that, right now, right here, in this book, because the truth has been gnawing at me for years *and today I break my silence!*

Dear Mrs. Alexander,

The day you returned our stories to us and told me that mine had real potential to be published, I was at once elated and ashamed. There was something in my story that wasn't true, and I need to confess it to you, here and now. I apologize for the lie. I did it to save face. I did most things, when I was eighteen years old, to save face. Oh, also, the story I turned in to you was not all of the story. My first date was full of pitfalls and peril and one super embarrassing moment when I accidentally choked on a carrot. But the ending? A climactic ending if there ever was one. Unfortunately, you did not get to hear about it because the assignment was to give you "3–5 pages" and so I gave you 3⅛ pages. I was, as you might recall, a "giver of the bare minimum." (I believe you called me that once.)

Yours truly,
Melissa Radke

So, without further ado, I give the world "My First Date" from Composition and Rhetoric, circa 1993.

EAT CAKE. BE BRAVE.

Melissa Lee   Narrative Essay

Composition & Rhetoric I   527 words

Sept. 22, 1993

My First Date

It was dark outside, and the air was slightly chilly. I sat completely motionless as I listened for the roar of the car to come up the gravel driveway. I heard nothing. The silence was deafening. As I sat on the edge of my bed, my heart pretending to be a racing time bomb, I was almost positive my room began to spin around me. I walked over to my bedroom window and peered through my mini-blinds one last time. But as the past had proven before, there was nothing. My nervousness began to grow. I looked at my watch, I looked at myself. I looked at myself, I looked at my watch. It had been only a short time but it seemed like hours. I left my room. I approached my mom, my eyes brimming with tears. I noticed the strangest thing, her eyes were also filling with tears. But what were they tears of? Joy? Anger? Sorrow? I couldn't understand her pain. I was the one standing on the edge of the unknown.

It seemed like such a dream, when I look back on it now. It seems like it was a million years ago, but yet I can still remember it like it was yesterday.

It was my freshman year in high school. The bell rang for my seventh period class. I was late getting out of my sixth period class, so as I rushed to my locker, the people around me all became a blur. I grabbed my books and headed for biology. "Hey there," I heard him say, only a few feet away. I couldn't turn around. My stomach wouldn't allow me to. Come to think of it, neither would my head, or my feet, etc. I pretty much seemed to lose all consciousness whenever he was around. I had all the classic symptoms, too. The hammering heart, the stomach that always seemed to take a skydive at just the right moment, and let's not forget my blind feet. They allowed me to run into anything and anybody within a fifty mile radius.

Nothing, I said absolutely nothing. Not "Hi, Hello, Greetings, Nice to see you, Do you know the mating ritual of the African grasshopper?" I was totally speechless. Besides, even if I had been able to say anything, it would have had to have been the word, "water." My mouth was so dry, it was beginning to feel a lot like Styrofoam. I did somehow manage a smile, however. "Where ya headed?" he asked, as if he actually had an inkling of a care. "Biology with Mr. Weems," I replied in a complete state of awe. "Let me walk ya there," he said as I slowly began to melt away. And so he did, and what happened during that moment is something I shall never forget.

He was eighteen years old, a senior who had been given every honor except a key to the city. He was everyone's friend, and every sports pro. He was incredible.

EAT CAKE. BE BRAVE.

As we approached the doorway of my biology class, I slightly detected an air of nervousness in his voice. "Shawn," I asked, "are you about to be sick?". I thought this was why he had become so antsy. He laughed and acted a little relieved after my obviously absurd question. "Uh, no, no, well, would you like to go with me to a Valentine party on Saturday night?" Suddenly it was as if slow motion had taken over the world, and a large cloud full of light, and a band of angels singing, came down from the heavens and transformed me into a mature, confident, thirty year old, that any relationship specialist would be proud of. "Why of course Shawn, I'd love to go with you."

And now, here I was. All dressed up and no place to go. The clock read 7:04P.M. He was now four minutes late. It was official, I had been stood up. I was in the depths of despair. My life from then on would be a graveyard of buried hopes and dreams. I sat down beside my mom who tried to console me with, "Don't worry, I remember when your dad..." stories. But I knew, as my heart sunk, that I had been forgotten, discarded. That was it, I was packing up my family and leaving town.

As I began to race over the dreams of how the night could have been, I heard a car. Not to seem to overzealous, I slowly walked to the window, but my heart had already beaten me there. The next thing I heard was a knock on the door. I t seemed to echo throughout the house.

As I turned to leave, I glanced back at my mom who was holding back the tears that I felt like using. I was nervous, I was afraid, I was on my first date.   *excited?*

Delightful essay, Melissa, capturing the universal feelings of puppy love and the first date. You have masterfully created the mood of teary nervousness as you wait for him, then you transport your reader to a high school hall and poetically describe the symptoms of love sickness. Your humor and creativity bring reality to this situation between boy and girl. And your exaggerated melancholy at his lateness makes your relief at his arrival more keenly felt. Your concluding sentence is memorable in its parallel form.

My main concern is grammar. You have written four comma splices with the second clauses beginning with "her," "it," and "I." Also, you fail to begin new paragraphs whenever you shift speakers.
I enjoyed reading this essay, Melissa. I think it has publishing possibilities.
Grade: 93/100 (Lowered due to comma splices)

Sweet, isn't it? He asked me out and then he got there late and I was nervous and my heart was beating out of my chest. Makes for a great read. Except none of it was true! Aside from the part where I was madly in love with him and I could barely talk when he walked by and all I heard in my head was Joey McIntyre singing "I'll Be Loving You Forever."

So, without further ado, I give the world the complete and honest story about my first date. From the dark recesses of my mind, circa 2017.

Melissa Radke Narrative Essay
Eat Cake. Be Brave. 2,184 words
November 9, 2017

My First Date: A Tyler Perry Production

It was dark outside and the air was supposed to have been chilly, considering it was February. But this was East Texas, so it was a balmy eighty-two degrees and I was sweating off my makeup. I sat in my room on my daybed and bit my fingernails as I waited for his car to come up the freshly poured cement driveway. (Not freshly poured as in that afternoon, but fresh enough that my dad still swept off dirt after anyone drove on it while repeating, "This driveway is a showpiece now, Annette, a showpiece.") I heard nothing. Of course, he had agreed to pick me up at six p.m. and it was 5:37 p.m., but where the heck was he? He wasn't coming! I knew it! As I sat on the edge of my bed, my heart burning from an acid reflux attack, I popped one of my dad's Rolaids and felt better almost instantly. I walked over to one of the posters that hung on every square inch of my room, New Kids on the Block, and looked deep into their eyes one last time. I thought I heard the rumble of his car but realized that was just my dad passing gas in the hallway. My nerves were a wreck. I looked at Donnie, I looked at Joey. I looked at Jordan, I looked at Jonathan. It was now 5:38 p.m. and I was starting to get kinda freaked.

I left my room and said, "Oh my gosh, Dad, it smells terrible in this hallway."

"I'm nervous, too, ya know?" he said as he apologized. I squirted more perfume on me. I approached my mom, my eyes glistening from the stench, when I noticed the strangest thing: Her eyes were beginning to tear up as well.

"What in the world did you put on?"

"*Electric Youth* by Debbie Gibson."

"Babe, you're gonna kill him!"

How could she say that to me? Didn't she know that I was sixteen and standing on the edge of the unknown?

I want to say that my first date seemed like a dream, and that as I look back on it, almost thirty years later, I can still remember it like it was yesterday. But none of that is true. My first date will always go down in my mind as the night my curfew was eleven p.m. but I was home by ten fifteen p.m. Also, I couldn't possibly remember every detail—I forget to pack my kids a lunch most days.

It was my freshman year in high school. The bell rang for my seventh-period class and I ran like a bat out of hell to get to it. I was not late getting out of my sixth-period class; as a matter of fact, I was purposely *never* late because that would mean I did not get to stalk my high school crush and magically appear in the same hall, walking the same pace, with him, every single day. I grabbed my books and headed for biology...I hated biology. "Hey there," I said to him just like I did every day. Every, sad, embarrassing, day. "Whatcha doin'?" Oh my word, why did I ask that? I am such an idiot. I know what he's doing, he's doing the same thing he does every day at this time and then again on Monday mornings at nine forty-five and Wednesday just before lunch. I pretty much seemed to lose consciousness when he was around, except for my keen predatory senses. Which is what I was, you know—a predator. I had all the classic stalking techniques mastered: waiting in the bushes, ability to pounce, sniffing out other predators within my line of vision, pretending to bump into him but then actually bumping into him so hard his books would drop.

"Oh, hi," he said. Did you hear that? He said "oh," as if seeing me was both a shock and a delight. I knew I was pulling this off!

"Where are you headed?" he asked.

"To biology with Mr. Weems. Man, I love biology. All the plankton and flora. Do you want to walk me there?"

"Well, I'm going that way anyway, so..."

"Great!"

And so he did, and what happened during that moment is something I shall never forget...mainly because I have lied about it for thirty years.

He was eighteen years old and a senior. He was a really nice guy and well liked on campus. I'm pretty sure he was good in sports, but I can't be positive. I mean, the closest I came to participating in a sport was that I sang in the choir. But I know he played baseball and made a lot of touchdowns, so that's good, right? What did I know about it?

As we approached the doorway of my biology class the scent of fermented pigs began to rise in my nose. Like a Southern belle nurse to Confederate soldiers, I was overcome with the vapors and began to throw up a little in my mouth. He must have noticed this because his next question to me was, "Are you okay? You look like you're about to be sick."

I tilted my head back and laughed at this absurd question. "Me? Sick? Are you...*dry heave*... kidding...*dry heave*...I'm all good." And then, right at the moment I was dry heaving and my biology teacher was rolling in another cart of dead pigs, I asked him to go with me to a Valentine banquet. That's right! What happened then is that *I asked him* out. I *freaking* asked him out. I loved him, and I was dry heaving and there were a bunch of dead pigs in the area and I asked him out like a complete loon. With all the graciousness he could muster, he looked me straight in the eye and said, "Absolutely. I'd love to go with you."

Now, here I was. All dressed up—in a dress my mother had made for me—and no place to go. It was 5:58 p.m. and I had clearly been stood...oh wait, nope, he's here. *Daaaaang*, and he's two minutes early. Talk about anxious! Guy just can't wait to be with me.

To not seem overzealous I slowly walked to the window, peered through the miniblinds and did some kind of dance that caused me to throw one of my hips out. The next thing I knew there was a knock at the door. "Melissa, let's go! He's here and your mom and I are trying to make a movie!" My dad's words seemed to echo throughout the house. I loved how we always kept it classy.

As I turned to leave I glanced back at my mom, who (I was almost sure) was starting to cry...nope, she was just adjusting one of her contacts while motioning to her watch and telling me to "hurry it up." I was nervous. I was excited. I was on my first date with *him*.

Coincidentally, this would also be my last date with him. Not because it went badly; it didn't. I thought we had a really nice time. We laughed and the chitchat was easy. Oh sure, I choked on a carrot at dinner but I made sure he knew that hey...that's a carrot I'm choking on...a carrot...that's a *vegetable*. So, I kept it real. He was kind and respectful, and when we ran into a mutual friend at the banquet, who started his conversation with, "Dang, my mom just had curtains made out of that same fabric, Melissa," he made sure to compliment how I looked. I could really see me marrying this guy, settling down, raising some kids, and having some chickens. I had drawn pictures of me marrying this guy, and I kid you not when I say that in the pictures we always had a bunch of kids and everyone was feeding chickens. I don't know why. The late eighties were weird for me.

On our way home he reached over and held my hand. I think I blacked out for a mile and a half. This moment came as the song "It Must Have Been Love" by Roxette began to play on the radio. Can you feel the power of such an intense eighties moment? If you can't, then I implore you, dear ones, to close your eyes, block out the laundry you are sitting beside, and imagine yourself in a car with your biggest high school crush. Now imagine he reaches over and grabs your hand right as Marie Fredriksson is banging out those high notes—"but it's *over now*"—and you tell me how life could get any more perfect. It couldn't!

As we made our way down my driveway we made small talk and laughed but I knew...I knew what was coming. I had walked in on my mom watching *Dallas* one night, so I knew exactly what was about to happen and I was prepared. I had prepared for this kiss for months! I had practiced my moves in the mirror and made a list of exactly how to do it without looking like someone who would make a list on how to do it. To say I was cool as a cucumber was putting it mildly. My heart was beating 108 beats a minute, give or take, although it's hard for you to take your pulse when someone is holding your other hand. Why had I not thrown this into the equation?

He must have seen me checking my pulse on my neck because he suddenly asked if I was okay.

"Me? I cool as cucumber. I am cool as cucumber. I. Am. As. Cool. As. A. Cucumber. There, that's what I was trying to say."

"But you're sweating."

I wiped my forehead and upper lip. "What? This? No, I'm not, I'm just perspiring. There's a big difference. It's probably the heat in the car."

He apologized and offered to turn it down, and in doing so he removed his hand. *What was wrong with me?* None of this had been on the list I had made, none of it. I calmed myself as we drove up the hill to my home...

(I would speak first. Every negotiator knows not to speak first, but I could not for the life of me remember one reason why that was important, so I spoke first.)

"Thank you for taking me tonight on my very first date."

"Oh my gosh, is it your first date?"

(Okay, now I see why speaking first is frowned upon.)

"Well, yeah, but hopefully not my last! I don't mean with you though. I mean, of course you but I don't mean 'of course, you,' you know what I mean? I am willing to go out with anyone. Ha! Not anyone, I don't even know why I said that."

(He's putting the car in park. Why is he putting the car in park? I can tuck and roll. I have tucked and rolled a few times before. That's a lie, I've never tucked and rolled, but I saw it on *T.J. Hooker* once, so I can probably do it.)

"Well, I'm honored to have taken you on your first—of many—dates. I had a very nice time. And now I know to watch out for those carrots."

(He made a joke. My mom says to laugh at their jokes because it lets them know you don't have to be the only funny person in the room, which is a turn-off.)

"Oh! The carrot! My gosh, the carrot! Boy, are you ever right. That carrot was something else. It really got lodged down in there. I was *this close* to throwing it up."

(Well played, Melissa.)

"Well, thanks again for asking me..."

(This is it. He's leaning in. He is *freaking fracking leaning in* and I cannot, oh my word his face is getting so close to mine, oh my oh my oh my oh my here it comes here it comes here it comes...I lean back.)

"You're welcome. Okay, I will see you at school."

I opened the car door and I did not remove my body gracefully, I hurled my body at a rapid rate out of the car and closed the door. I was alive. The date was over and I was alive and I was upright. I was upright with only one shoe on, but still, I was upright.

(Where is my shoe? What happened to my shoe? Oh no, my shoe is in the car.)

I turned and opened the car door. He was frozen, his body still leaning over, but his eyes were locked on me.

"I am so sorry. I think my shoe...oh yes, there it is. Right here in your floorboard. Can't leave that. Got it! Okay, thanks again!"

I closed the door and saw him move. Finally, he put

the car in reverse and pulled out of my driveway. I walked into my room, lay down on my bed, and cried myself to sleep.

And that, Mrs. Alexander, is the real and true story behind my first date.

Any idea why a chubby incoming freshman might not want to share the truth?

Any idea why the story I wanted to read to the entire class starred me as the desirable one?

Did you know, Mrs. Alexander, that it would be four more years before I would finally have that first kiss? And it would not be with my high school crush, the man I obsessed over for four long years in high school and whose name I wrote all over my notebooks and on the back of my bedroom door *"in pen,"* as my dad likes to remind me. It would be with a boy who sat right there in that Composition and Rhetoric class and listened to me read that story. It would be with that boy who after class walked up beside me and said, "No way that story is true. You're too much of a mess for it to have gone down that way." I told him to "shut up and keep walking, Radke." But he kept coming around, Mrs. Alexander. Until one day, much like the fictional story I crafted for you, he asked me out. And guess what? His mouth got dry and shaky as he started to sweat when he told me how he felt, just like mine had a few years prior. And soon, Mrs. Alexander, he would lean in for a kiss and I would, too;

I wouldn't run, or bail, and this time I kept both feet firmly on the ground...and in my shoes. My first kiss would be with an idiot jerk I sat next to in your class named David Radke. I would marry him one year later, Mrs. Alexander, and as mortified as I was for jumping out of the car that Valentine night of 1989, I am most happy that the first kiss I ever had was with the only man I've ever loved.

And *that's* a true story.

Dedicated to Shawn.
My first crush. My first date. My sweet friend.
(*But you ain't nooooo David Radke.*)

Chapter 8

Let's Just Talk about the Cover, Shall We?

Hello, Melissa.

For now, I'd like to share an idea we have for the cover. Think of the iconic Audrey Hepburn/Holly Golightly. We'd love to style you exactly like that. But no cigarette holder and instead maybe holding a cake slicer or a giant fork or something like that. Or like Marilyn Monroe in the bathtub from *The Seven Year Itch*. Or like a Greek goddess. Imagine that with the title: *Eat Cake. Be Brave.* You are taking a classic image of beauty and what all women are supposed to want to be, and making it into your own, plus combined with the title, says exactly what the book's message is. That cover photo will be striking, powerful, arresting, and also off-kilter to go with your sense of humor. It's the kind of cover that the media will eat up, which would be a great thing! I discussed this cover idea today in a meeting with my publisher, the associate publisher/director of marketing, and our sales director—and they all loved it as much as I do.

Mull it over and shoot me an email or a text or call me and we can discuss further.

Beth

———

Dear Beth,

Is someone in your office holding you hostage? Is this your attempt at screaming for help? If you are unable to dial 911, then just email me back the phrase "No one wants to see you in sleeveless" and I will do all I can to get help to you and your co-workers!

Melissa

Dear Melissa,

No one is holding me hostage. We are all just fine. I would thank you for your concern but I didn't feel like it was sincere. So, are we good to go on the cover?

Beth

Beth,

The last time I went sleeveless was in 2001, and that was because I was spending the entire day at Dollywood during the month of September. They took one of those pictures of us mid-ride on a roller coaster. My dad and my sister are screaming with laughter, but right behind them are David and me. I have a horrific look on my face, whereas he looks like he is being hit in the face with a chicken breast. It was my upper arm. That said, I'm going to ask that you reconsider this option or that you immediately check yourself into one of those places that lets you rest and meditate and serves smoothies at breakfast.

Melissa

My dear Melissa,

I am your editor and you know I will deal with you completely honestly, right? So here is my complete honesty: You are holding us up with this back-and-forth. Are you going to do the cover like Audrey Hepburn/Marilyn Monroe/Greek goddess or not?

Beth

Sweet, sweet, tiny Beth,

You love my back-and-forth and you know it. One of the reasons why you wanted to sign me was because I was exceptionally dramatic and demanded an intensely high amount of validation and praise. Am I wrong about that? Be honest...

Melissa

Dear Drama Queen,

You are wrong. Terribly wrong. The reason I wanted to sign you was because of your potential to write a best seller, which would help me pay off the pool I want to put in my backyard, but the longer I spend with you the less likely I see either of those things happening. The book cover is happening in 3...2...

Beth

Uhhhhhh, Beth, you would be the worst hostage negotiator in the world! Also, the joke's on you, because I have no plans on writing a best seller *and* if you make me wear sleeveless then I hope that pool never happens and your children have to run through a sprinkler like I did when I was growing up! (Except I didn't run through a sprinkler because I didn't run. So, ha! Joke's on you...again!)

Melissa

Dear Melissa,

. . . 1.

Thanks,
Beth

———✦———

Beth,

DANGIT!

Melissa

———✦———

And that, my lovelies, is how that front cover came to be. You thought it was going to be glamorous, right, with a lot of talking over a conference table and someone bringing us espressos?

Nope.

It happened over email while I was dropping my dogs off at the groomer's, which is why I do not feel like I represented myself very well. Had I had my wits about me I would have fought a little harder for less glamour, more lumberjack. Less Audrey Hepburn/MM/Greek goddess, more Kathy Bates. But she wouldn't hear it. The team *(that's right, I have a "team"; don't hate)* felt strongly that my insecurities and disastrously low amount of dignity would be a huge draw for travelers racing to catch a flight in airport bookstores around the world. *Fingers crossed!*

What they didn't know—up until the moment they edited this book—was this: I felt very strongly that I did not want to wear sleeveless on the cover. Or a dress on the cover. Or even *be* on the cover. And then—*snap!*—just like that, I felt very strongly that I did. Not because my arms had changed, but because my perspective had.

Listen, I didn't wear $1,400 worth of Spanx for you. I did it for me.

I did it because to put so much emphasis and brain power and Ativan on what I might look like on the outside is to put zero confidence in the words that make up the inside. I know that the truth inside this book is worth more than my shoulders or chins. I would risk sleeveless again and again and again if it meant you would be intrigued enough to pick this book up and read truth. We are past perfection! Way past it. We are a world made up of brilliant, strong, truth-telling, mountain-scaling, award-winning, child-bearing women who love a good pair of skinny jeans as long as they have a horrific amount of stretch in them. We are not ashamed or embarrassed anymore. We don't have to be!

If I had my way I would have taken a picture draped in an oversized sweater standing in my backyard, with a scarf that covered half my face and only my eyes showing.

But I couldn't.

I couldn't tell you to be brave and then hide.

I couldn't ask you to step up and then slink back.

I couldn't tell you that your worth was grand and elaborate and too extravagant for you to even imagine, only to dismiss my own.

So, I showed up. Okay, that makes it sound like it was all so simple. It wasn't. I ate low carb for three weeks before. I got my roots done and eyelash extensions put on. I did a charcoal mask on my face every night for a week. I cried the entire day before, and I had everyone in my family and circle of friends praying for me and on personal stand-by. But I showed up! I walked in, I met a stylist and a makeup artist, a photographer and an assistant, and I never apologized for one ounce of me. I never expressed regret for one dress that didn't fit or one zit that couldn't be covered or my left boob being significantly—*significantly*—lower than the right.

Sometimes you just have to show up. Fear and all. Nerves and all. Heck, bring them with you! They are real, and so are you. Friend, you can look in the mirror all day long, repeat the phrase *I will not be scared* until the cows come home, throw salt over your shoulder, and avoid every crack on the sidewalk, but you are still going to walk in a bit shaky.

But you walked in . . . and that's what matters.

I suggest that you look in the mirror and say this:

No one thinks I will.

No one thinks I can.

But I know better.

Sure, I'm wearing a body girdle that would kill a medium-sized man—

and yes, my pants may or may not have an elastic waist in them.

But dang, I look good!

I feel even better.

Will I walk in without fear? Probably not.

But once I'm there I will make fear sit down and be my little *beyotch*,

because this I can tell you, God has given me a lot of things, but not one of them is fear.

He's given me this head on my shoulders and the ability to have really incredible hair.

He's given me a swing in my hips and a strut in my walk.

He's given me a butt that won't quit and a chest most men would pay a subscription for.

But He has *not* given me fear.

So, with all the power He has lent me,

all the love He has shown me,

and all the sanity I can muster,

I will just. *Freakin'. Show. Up.*

And then go and do it. In fact, *kill it.*

Chapter 9

This Is Where I Went off the Rails and Started Melting My M&M's.

I flunked out of the first college I ever went to. *Okay? You happy?*

There. Now that that's out of the way...

I'm sorry, what did you ask? *What did I flunk?* I flunked history. Which I suppose means I'm doomed to repeat it.

I was supposed to go to college in Missouri, but one month before I was set to leave my parents decided a college closer to home was a better idea in case I "got homesick" or "needed something" or "wanted to drive home for a visit."

What in the world were they talking about?

Were they joking?

I was so ready to leave home that I was like a calf at the starting gate, wide-eyed and totally confused but still ready to bust outta there.

Fast-forward to day 3 of college: Did you know that if you cry in the shower no one can hear you and your tears and snot require no tissues so you're even saving trees?

Oh yeah, real self-reliant there, Melissa. What a big-shot college girl I was, huh? My biggest concerns my first week of college? *How long until I could go home and see my parents and maybe Dad would go to Blockbuster and rent us a movie and I wonder if Mom might make chicken salad.*

(I'm embarrassed even writing that last sentence.)

Around day 4 or 5 of my Great College Experience, a girl stopped me and my awesome shower caddy in the hall and asked, "Okay, Melissa, what is up with you? You are taking two or three showers a day. Is everything alright?"

I explained that I was fine and showers were awesome and who wouldn't want to take a shower in shower stall 2 with its hair-in-the-drain charm and shower shoe coolness?

"Wait. Are you taking showers in right showers or left showers?"

"Left showers."

"Ohhhhhh myyyy gawd, so there's nothing wrong with you—you're just a clean freak."

"No, there *is* something wrong with me. I miss my . . ."

"Right. Okay. Cool. But there's nothing like freaky

wrong with you! *Whew.* Load off. I can let the girls know. That's a relief. Cry on, Mel!" she said as she headed down the hall.

I had no clue what she was talking about, but as my shower shoes and I made our way to the communal bathrooms I decided to see for myself the difference in left showers and right showers. Maybe she was on to something; I had not seen very many girls use the left showers, but I like to blaze my own trail. I'm cool like that.

I walked into the bathroom and turned right. I picked the first shower on the right side. I stepped in, turned the water on, closed my eyes, leaned my head back, let the water fall over my face, and started to cry. I wiped the water from my eyes and turned around, and it was then that I saw his picture. It was a school yearbook picture, nothing special, but it wasn't a small wallet size by any means. He was cute, really cute, and so all-American looking, kind of like Matt Damon before we knew who Matt Damon was. And there he was, hanging on the wall of a right shower. He was the reason every upperclassman on my hall used right showers. He was the reason they thought I was showering three times a day. I looked at his picture and started to laugh. It might have been the first time I had truly laughed since I'd been away from home. (Thank you, Richard. You weren't at all my type, but it was the first time I had taken a shower at college and not cried, so I'll give you that.)

I turned the water off, grabbed my towel, and wondered if he had any idea they put his picture up in shower 1, right side. I stepped out of the shower and four girls from my hall began to clap.

"You did it. You took a shower without crying for chicken salad!" one of them said.

"Wait. You all have been able to hear me?"

"They're not soundproof, for God's sake. Welcome to college, Melissa. There's more where that came from." And with that they took my hand, led me down the hall, and invited me to watch what would inevitably cause me to flunk history: *Melrose Place.*

———————

College was the anti–high school. The friends I made were creative and dramatic and eclectic. They wore palazzo pants. And mules! They were older than I was and they read *Cosmopolitan* magazine and aced all the quizzes. Their earrings were huge! Their lipstick was called Cherries in the Snow, and when they wore overalls, they left one side undone. It was the most fashionable place I had ever been. The nineties were looking up!

My college experience was a great one. Maybe a little too great. As much fun as I had during the day—when classes were supposed to be going on—at night I had tenfold, roaming the halls, popping in on almost everyone to chat about their day, their date, and why my new haircut still had not made my face look a thing like Josie

Bissett's. Night after night I would put on my pajamas, leave my dorm room, and make my rounds from 1st South to 2nd South to 1st North and 2nd North. I was like your friendly neighborhood crime prevention expert, but with a FRANKIE SAY RELAX nightshirt on and no bra.

When I think back to that time in my life, I have narrowed it down to the three types of women who go to college:

1. Those who excel.
2. Those who have too much fun.
3. Those who get fat.

I was a hard two closing in on a super-size three, if you know what I'm saying.

Around week 6, I discovered the vending machines in our building. This was big news! After all, this was the nineties; there was no Amazon Prime delivering groceries to our door. If we wanted snacks, we had to count change and press A3 like all the other hardworking folk. They had M&M's. Five different vending machines and every one of them had M&M's. Every night, before I made my rounds, I took all the money I could scrounge up and made my purchase. I would pour bags of M&M's into a paper cup—full to the top—and microwave them. If you are reading this and thinking, *That Melissa is so crazy, my goodness, a cup full of candy every night? Silly girl!* then I need you to be less that and more *Dear Lord! A cup full of M&M's every single night? What was wrong? Someone please, call a hotline number or something; our girl is slipping.*

I would like to tell you that I have learned and grown and that I no longer turn to chocolate to comfort myself, but I signed a contract that I would be honest in this book. *(Note to self: Find a new attorney.)* Of course, I still pull out the chocolate when I can't get in to see my therapist for another week; doesn't everyone?

But if I'm being honest, I'm not sure it was just the M&M's that were the problem.

When I arrived at college I had a head full of long blond hair down to the middle of my back. One month into school I was sporting a Halle Berry pixie cut. When the hairstylist asked me if I was totally sure before he made his first big chop with those scissors, I replied, "Absolutely! Momma's got a new pair of shoes." To this day, I have no idea what that even means.

It was one thing to skip a class, but I would skip days and days of classes. There would be entire weeks I would not attend a single class. My parents still do not know this, so please don't tell them.

Another unhealthy thing: I saw *The Bodyguard*—in the theater—five times! When my friends asked me why I had seen it so many times, I told them that I wasn't sure but whenever I watched Kevin Costner "I got a really funny feeling in my pants." They explained what that was, too, because *#sheltered*. By the time the ruggedly handsome Kevin Costner (and ol' whatshername) left the theaters, I had purchased the cassette tape, hung up posters in my dorm, and located his house on a map of the stars brochure I found once in an airport bathroom.

Are you starting to see a pattern here? I certainly was. College brought something out in me that I had not seen before and it was this: There was no in-between for me.

No gray areas. No blurry lines.

No self-control, self-restraint, or self-discipline.

I was all or nothing. I was extreme.

I was either heating up eight bags of M&M's a night or starving myself for an entire weekend in order to lose a quick forty-six pounds. I was either completely obsessed with Kevin Costner or I was...actually, there's no real opposing position for that. But you get what I'm saying.

One of my best friends once described me as "Melissa is the girl whose house you toilet paper on a Friday night—and she hangs your cat from a ceiling fan on Sunday." Of course, he's an idiot, as I have never murdered a cat. But he isn't totally wrong. If I love you, I love you all the way and forever. If you wrong me, I will look up your grandmother's address. I'm not proud of this, and even at the time of this writing I struggle with it still, in certain areas. The word is *moderation*, and I have a deficit.

———

Melissa, I am sorry to interrupt you right now but you gave me this chapter to read and I could only get so far before I had to hand it to your daddy and go lie in my bed and grieve myself to death, so I hope you're happy, you do know I'm in my sixties and all my friends are going to read this and find out that you showered with a boy's picture like some kind of nutcase! And don't even get me started on that bit about Kevin Costner as you have certainly soiled that name in my house forever—which makes me upset because you know how me and your aunt Melba feel about him, I'm not even sure how I will be able to even tell your granny about this, we can only hope she's home with Jesus before this heartache hits the shelves. But that is not my main reason for writing to you about this chapter, it is because you said college brought something out of you that you had not seen before but maybe you should have interviewed me and asked me if I had seen it before because nobody knows you like your momma knows you and I am here to tell you I most certainly had seen it, I saw it all of your life but especially those last couple of years you were in high school, oh baby, it was such a horrible time for you what with your acne and inability to lose any weight at all but I digress because that is not the thing we are talking about right now. The thing I am referring to right now was your inability to self-regulate or understand moderation at all. Oh honey, let me tell you something, it was so horrible that your daddy and I honestly thought you might be worshipping the devil or something because you know some of them had moved into our town? It was the way you acted and you had zero self-control, Melissa Paige, zip/zero/none, but now baby, you know I'm just being honest when I say that moderation has always been a problem for you, don't you go off pouting at my saying that. Do you remember the time you walked in my front door and your beautiful blond hair was jet black and you looked just like Snow White? Why, we all just assumed you had gotten a part in *Madama Butterfly*, you always did love the theater. Or what about the time you got sideways with me and put a whole dead chicken way up high in my kitchen cabinet for two whole months during the heat of the summer? Melissa Paige, that's not normal behavior! We had to call in professionals to figure out what the smell was, I'll have you know...but baby the problem wasn't just with your hair or your grades or that whole dead chicken. The problem was in your inability to measure the emotional output given to certain situations. I hope you even understand what I'm saying, I heard Dr. Phil say that one time so that's why I'm saying it. But it's like the time you went out to eat with your girlfriends and you had to take your Nutrisystem shake but they were all able to order pasta, and what did you do? You tossed a chair across the room, Melissa Paige. You can see why we were just sure you were worshipping the devil. So are you seeing my point here? I know it hurts but Momma always knows the truth and I want you to really try and do better okay? And Melissa, please remove the part about Kevin Costner, you know how much your daddy loves *Dances with Wolves.*

———◁≡

That was my mom, y'all. (When your editor suggests you let those "close to you" read your chapters first, they are just trying to hurt you.)

Truth is, she's right. My inability to moderate my feelings, emotions, or responses has been an issue for me for years. It's the reason why I can love so much but can also hurt so deeply (and whether you read that as *I can hurt people so deeply* or *I can get hurt so deeply*, you're right). It's why I didn't gain the freshman fifteen but gained the freshman fifty. It's why when I am upright I have a ton of friends, but if I am off or angry, suspect, or paranoid, I can annihilate them in an instant—leaving me lonely and playing the role of victim. It is why I don't often want to answer for my actions or address my inner conflicts. Because I am afraid that maybe, just maybe, the problem lies with me.

Author Glennon Doyle is quoted as saying, "I understand now that I am not a mess but a deeply feeling person in a messy world." I love that quote. I wish to the heavens it were true for me. But it's not. Truth is, unlike her, I am just a mess. I am a hot mess. I am a hot mess in a hot mess of a world and neither of us is doing the other any favors.

Let's Oprah the crap out of that comment one more time: *I am a hot mess. I am a hot mess in a hot mess of a world, and neither of us is doing the other any favors.*

I discovered this about myself many years ago, and I feared I might be beyond repair. I dreaded the long look inside myself, the actual introspection. I, in no way, felt strong enough to do the kind of personal self-examination that this task required. So, now what? Where do I go?

I could find a new therapist.

I could buy another book.

I could record Dr. Phil...again.

I could go lie on a beach.

I could go on a hike.

I could do a cleanse.

I could do a fast.

Or I could start with the one who created me, the one who created each fiber and counted each hair, who placed every interest and desire and passion in my DNA. The one who formed my thoughts and designed my emotions, who knew my fears and has always been very aware of my inadequacies. The one who looked into my newly formed eyes on the day I was completed and said, "Done. Look at her. I like this one. I like this one a lot. She's interesting."

So. I decided to start there.

Chapter 10

It's the Old Mermaid–Tinker Bell–Rose Lamp.

I remember the day my mom brought it home. She walked in with it behind her back and then revealed it as if it was something we had been looking forward to, something we had been waiting on. I promise you, no one was waiting on this lamp. If anyone had been doing any "waiting," then it had to be the owners of the furniture store she had purchased it from. They'd been waiting on a sucker, and they had finally found one in my mom.

"*Henry, you drove to a market show and this is what you bring back to the store?*"

"*Trust me, Eunice, someone will buy this. There is one born every minute.*"

"So, what do we do until they're born?"

"We wait."

Or at least that's how I imagined that conversation going. I'm probably right.

My dad slunk in behind her looking guilty, looking sorry. He should have been sorry! He purchased this for her, so it served him right that he would have to look at it for the next forty years. But what about me? What had I done wrong? I didn't deserve this.

She held up the lamp and asked if I thought it was as pretty as she did.

"I'm confused. Are you asking if I think the lamp is as pretty as you are? Or are you asking if I think the lamp is as pretty as you think you are? Or are you wanting to know if the lamp is as pretty as you think the lamp is in comparison to how attractive you are?"

"Melissa Paige, go to your room."

I couldn't spend my life in my room, so I decided to accept the lamp. I decided to accept it staring at me as I walked in and out of a room. I decided to accept that it was neither a flower nor a mermaid. It wasn't even really a lamp for that matter. Yet somehow it was all of those things when taken together. Out of the stem of the gigantic flower came a mermaid's head, and at the base where, you know, logically, a stem would be—were fins. There was no lampshade, only a ceramic flower that the lightbulb screwed into. Accepting these facts meant accepting that, based off of her purchase of this lamp alone, my mom was going blind. Or crazy. The jury is still out on both of those things.

Oh, but the attention the Mermaid–Tinker Bell–Rose lamp brought to our family. I'm not sure why we never made it into one of those "day trips in Texas" books tourists can buy, but I really think we should have. We could have charged those tourists a quarter for a cup of sweet tea to sip while they walked around our house looking awkwardly at my mom's family room filled with nothing but black baby dolls wearing overalls or holding fishing poles, and finally ending up at the lamp, where they would take pictures and create a memory that would last them for years. Don't say I didn't try to bring big business to deep East Texas!

My parents' friends would come over and look at it and say things like, "Hey, Larry, get a picture of me holding the lamp!" I once heard one of my dad's buddies say, "Why, Gene, why?" All he said back was, "I love her." That hideous lamp sat in my parents' living room for almost fifteen years. She never regretted that forty-eight-dollar purchase for one minute.

One year into my marriage, David and I moved into a new townhome in Nashville that we thought was very fancy and very spacious. Come to find out it was not a great area, and our neighbors were arrested for running a prostitution ring inside their home, but I digress...I needed things to fill up the ample amount of space, and guess what my mom offered me? That's right, the lamp.

And like the idiot before me whom I affectionately refer to as Dad, I said yes. Mom made sure to pack up the lamp tightly in bubble wrap, lest any part of the mermaid's blond hair, which covers her naked breasts, get messed up in shipping. I opened it, found a place for it in my living room, and plugged it in.

It was still ugly.

But it was also home.

Nashville is a far drive from Texas, and sometimes the things you would think might never remind you of home do, and that's reason enough right there to set them out, plug them in, and let people point.

The Mermaid–Tinker Bell–Rose lamp lived in our townhouse for almost four years. After that we decided to purchase a small home, and I set the lamp in the corner under a sign that read TO BE PACKED—NEED BUBBLE WRAP—BE CAREFUL! No one reads my signs. Every few days I would find her bumped over, a piece chipped off and lying in the corner. With great effort, I picked up every chipped piece off of the floor and kept them in a clear sandwich bag, because I'm nothing if not classy. But the years had done some damage to Tink, and she was starting to show signs of aging, which is actually pretty remarkable if you think about it, because she had a great figure for someone born half flower, half mythical sea goddess, half electrical unit.

A couple of weeks before the movers were scheduled to come the lamp had still not been packed up. David did this on purpose, I have very little doubt. She had taken a beating and so many tiny pieces of her were being held in a clear plastic bag I hadn't managed to misplace (of all the things). I took the bag and the lamp to David and said, "If you love me, you will take her and get her fixed."

"Where am I supposed to do that?"

"A lamp restorer. I'm sure there are a ton around here."

"Do you know of any personally? I mean have you seen a sign or heard murmurings about a great lamp restorer? Because my gut says you're full of crap."

"David. Just take her to a place that does crafts—they'll know what to do!"

I showed him I meant business by wearing something seductive when I made this request. However, there is a very real chance he would have been so turned on he might not have even remembered what I had asked, which is why I had to tone it down by also eating a bowl of cereal while wearing it. It's called balance.

David and I began making trips to the new house, and we'd knock the lamp over.

Friends came over to help us make a few trips, and they'd knock the lamp over.

The movers came and they all but threw her into the street and lit her on fire.

She was having a rough time; it was written all over her...stem.

It was the last day, and almost everything had been moved out of the townhome and into our new place. Except for that one corner that still holds the stuff you never got packed up: the fancy crystal dish your aunt gave you at your wedding that you'll never use because you aren't Queen Elizabeth; five random CDs that you can't find the cases to; twelve beach towels, which is weird because you don't own a pool or live near a beach; a Mermaid–Tinker Bell–Rose lamp; and a tiny guitar from when you sat up late watching infomercials and swore you would learn to play it.

And then, because I'm me and I make terrible choices when I'm hungry, I walked over and threw them all away. Dumped every one of them in a big black trash bag and walked them out to the Dumpster. Those beach towels weren't mine! The CDs had scratches on them (plus something in my gut told me CDs would one day be irrelevant. I've always been ahead of my time). Why was that guitar so tiny? That crystal bowl looked stupid in a kitchen full of paper plates. And the lamp would never get fixed and never look whole again, so why bother! I dumped them into the large green bin and drove away. I didn't give it a second thought.

David and I had been settled into our new home for almost two months. Oh sure, there were still boxes sitting in the garage, unpacked, but that would be the case for another three years. What we needed was unpacked and in its rightful place, and I was feeling at home in our new little space when the phone rang.

"Is David Radke in?"

"No, he's not here right now. May I take a message?"

"Yeah, uhhh, this is Jim from Leipers Fork Antiques. Can you tell him I was able to locate the instrument we needed to fix the lamp, so he can bring it back in any-time."

"Oh. Uh. He brought it in?"

"Yeah, brought it in a while back. We made him take it back home, though, because we didn't think we'd be able to find what was needed to fix those tiny pieces, but we did. Just the instrument itself cost about fourteen hundred dollars, though."

"Fourteen hundred dollars? Are you kidding me?"

"No, ma'am. But did he tell you about the lamp? Fourteen hundred dollars is a drop in the bucket—the thing is probably worth about four thousand dollars. It's an incredible lamp. We'd still like to buy it from him, but he said you probably wouldn't want to part with it. But just think about it, okay? Anyway, tell him we called and he can bring it back in anytime."

He hung up.

———⋙

I've thought about that lamp a lot since that day. A whole lot. Do I wish I would have kept it? Of course I do. Is it because my husband did a very kind and romantic thing and not only took it to be looked at and fixed, but also brought it home and put it right back where it had been, making me none the wiser? Of course, that is one of the reasons. Is the larger reason that it was worth around four thousand dollars? Yes, it is much, much more that reason than anything else. Do I wonder how it ended up being that my mom—who from 1982 to 1988 decorated our house in the most politically incorrect ways you could imagine—found a lamp on a clearance rack at a small-town furniture store and brought it home for forty-eight dollars? I absolutely wonder that. I spent four months last summer labeling everything in her jewelry box with a neon orange tag, and it will be my luck that there isn't anything in there not purchased from the Christmas clearance on Jewelry TV—but the lamp we once tried to throw in a well and call a "witch" is worth thousands of dollars.

It's human nature to wonder those things. But had I not thrown it out, had I boxed up the lamp and sold it and pocketed the money, I would not have this story to share with you today. In fact, my story would end much like every other one of my stories:

Woman comes into money.

Woman buys new sunglasses because she sat on the other ones.

Woman enjoys a number 4 chicken meal when she usually only gets to have the number 3.

Woman goes home with twenty-seven cents in change.

But that isn't how this story ends. Something about this story is different. I think that's the point; I think this story was always supposed to be different and was always supposed to happen to me. I now believe the ol' Mermaid–Tinker Bell–Rose lamp was always supposed to come to me and leave me so that I would have to stew on it and pout about it. So that I would have to admit it to my husband. So that I would have to make sense of it.

And I have. Finally, I have.

———————

We throw out those things in the corner.

The things that don't fit into the regulated boxes. You know: KITCHEN, MASTER BEDROOM, LAUNDRY ROOM. Where do you put beach towels you've never seen, a guitar that barely fits in your hand, a crystal bowl, and a stack of famous TV theme song CDs? Where do you put a lamp that never really fit anywhere, anyway?

We dump those things. We gather them all up together and tie them safely so they don't escape. We drag them to the closest place we find that takes odd things and then we go back to our boxes that are nicely labeled and packaged and taped. We fill our homes with things that fit and look nice and no one points at or takes pictures of. If we are really lucky we fill our homes—and our heads and our hearts—with all of the Target things, all of the things everyone else has, so nothing about us really looks that different and nothing stands out and nothing needs to be explained away except to maybe say, "Oh, thank you! No, Target actually. Forty percent off, as a matter of fact. That's right, your girl likes a good bargain, I must confess."

Nothing stared at.

Nothing pointed at.

Nothing explained away.

And only after we are older and grown and looking at our life from a respectable distance do we even realize that we were one of the two things mentioned in this story: We were the tosser, or we were the lamp.

Oh, you evicters of misfits and unique finds.

You discarders and dismissers of worth.

You assumed because the paint was chipped off that the product was lacking.

You looked at something and because you couldn't explain it—you released it.

You saw something that looked like nothing. It sat in your way; it was high maintenance and would have required extra care, extra packaging.

Hey, I get it! Guilty as charged. You don't see a picture of me holding that lamp today, do you?

But what about you?

You tossed a friend.

You refused a sister.

You decided the relationship that you would have had to invest in was not worth the space it took up.

You dismissed an idea.

You rejected a love.

You turned your back on a neighbor.

And you wonder why everything in your home—and your head and your heart—looks exactly like everyone else's. It's because never once did you think value could be found in broken things; you took a clearance tag as the final word. My heart breaks for the things you might have passed over, the friendships you might have fixed, the relationships you could have salvaged. I wonder if you think about those things, like I think about that lamp. But alas, this book is not for you.

This book...this book is for the lamps.

(All my lamps out there, put your hands up!)

To the girls who looked different. Who didn't quite fit into the mold because some days you wanted to be a mermaid and some days you wanted to be Tinker Bell and some days you wanted to be a rose and, heck, some days you wanted to be all three at once. To the girls who were stared at or made fun of, whose voices were loud and whose ideas were different. Who never matched and never cared. It's for anyone who ever heard "you can't," "you really shouldn't," or "it's just not for you." It's for any lamp who has heard "you have such a beautiful face" so many times you thought you might barf. And it's for all those who have sat in the corner for far too long. Who have been pushed over and pushed aside. Who have chips and dings and scars in their skin, but are still in one piece...and still lightin' it up.

It was always about you.

This lesson was always about you.

It was about how we place an instant value amount on what we see. Not what we know about you or what we discover about you, and not how you make us feel or think or dream or learn or philosophize or dance. But what we see. And then—*and then*—we deduct from that amount the baggage that comes with each of us:

- Divorce? Deduction.
- Infidelity? Deduction.
- Abortion? Deduction.
- In debt? Deduction.
- A sordid past? Get out your calculator, this one's gonna cost...

Oh, but my dear lamp with your ceramic stem and your mermaid tail, you just haven't gotten the call; you, my friend, have yet to pick up the phone and talk to the fixer. What if I told you that what was broken on you did not have to stay that way? What if I told you that the stain from your past or your family or your weight or your health was no indicator of your worth? That you simply had yet to talk to the one who had all the right tools? The one who saw great worth in you. Not because you were a project, not because you were a hobby, but because you were valuable. Because *you are valuable*.

Let me take a minute and tell you what fixers do. You might think they just fix whatever they see that needs changing. Oh my, no! Their eye is incredible, and it's drawn to each tiny detail. Do they fix what is broken? Yes. They do not, however, fix what is different. They understand that what is broken makes you weak, but what is different makes you valuable.

The difference between the fixer and most everyone else? The fixer gets this.

It took me a long time to forgive myself for tossing that lamp. Not because I wanted that money, but because I felt as if I had tossed a piece of my own worth. That lamp, with its green petals and creepy undertones, resonated with me. And I junked it. But then the fixer called, and that's when the story changed. That's when, for me, it became less about the lamp and more about the lesson, less about the brokenness and more about the beauty.

May your mermaid heart leap at the thought that what has always made you different has, in fact, always made you priceless. Stay lit, my friends.

Chapter 11

Tiny Dancers. Tiny Cells.

I want you to take a breather.

Take a time out.

When my kids were little we had them sit on the "monkey mat" and think about how they were acting. I want you to take a seat there now. *Don't make me tell you again.*

You are spinning out of control.

Take a moment. Let your arms drop to your sides; you can even let your back slump a little. Slide your tap shoes off and count to ten. Let your hair down. Take your makeup off. Yes, *concealer, too.* You are performing yourself to death, darling. It doesn't have to be this way.

Listen to me, you can make jazz hands until the cows come home; it won't help. You will not change their minds about you. You will not convince them to see you any other way than the way they see you now.

This is not television. There is no plot twist.

No *Saved by the Bell* ending.

No *Bridget Jones* rom-com wrap-up.

I wish I was wrong, but I'm not.

What we have here is an impasse. *You are who you are, and who you are is not enough for them.*

Hear what I said: It's not enough *for them.*

I hate the way those words taste in my mouth, but I have too much of my mother in me to not be totally honest with you. You are not enough for them, baby, and there is a 99 percent chance that you never will be. Now, you can certainly keep at it. You can keep trying to be enough. No one is stopping you. You can lose the weight and grow the hair, fill the boobs and fix the nose. You can wear the heels and speak the words and dance the dance and play the game. Through blisters, corn pads, ulcers, and bloody toes you can tap dance your life away... if that's what you want.

But I don't think it is.

I know I don't want that for you.

What do I want? I want you to know—deep down in your bones—what "enough" feels like.

The difficult part in writing this chapter is that I am raising a daughter. At the ripe old age of eleven, she wears the same pair of high-top red Converse every day of her life because you never know when a pick-up game of wall ball might happen. She always looks like she just climbed down out of a tree. The first crush she ever had asked her what she wanted as a Valentine and she replied, confidently, "A thirty-dollar gift card to Red Lobster." The only thing she carries in her purse is a plastic cell phone full of candy, some ChapStick, and the bones of a lizard. I want to raise her strong; I want to raise her tough. If she wants something, I want her to go for it, try for it. If she doesn't get it the first time, I want her to know that she's capable of getting better at it, and then try again.

But I also want her whole.

I want her to know when enough is enough.

I want her to know when it is more important to protect the heart than make the squad.

This is a hard thing to teach in a world that applauds relentlessness. But mark my words, we will lose all the girls if we teach them that never stopping equals strength. I don't want to lose all the girls. I want our daughters healthy and capable and whole. I want them to know that when we stop to realize we are not enough for some, we are becoming perfectly enough for—you guessed it—*ourselves*.

Let me give you some examples.

NOT ENOUGH

They are right. Eventually the student does, indeed, become the teacher. At the time this story happened, I was a student. But look at me now, teaching the crap out of this to you knuckleheads.

It was 1999 and I was a student at Belmont University—a great school with a reputable music program in the center of the country music scene that is Nashville, Tennessee. My teacher first heard me sing at my senior recital; from that moment on he was a fan...and he was a fan of very few people. Except himself. I think he was a huge fan of himself. But I digress...

Our class was held in a large room overlooking Music Row, the make-or-break street in Music City. Home to publishing companies, record labels, and studios, Music Row was a popular destination in Nashville. You signed with the labels on the Row, and your songs were published on the Row, you recorded on the Row, and you had important meetings at Pancake Pantry...which was one block over from the Row. It all happened on the Row, he said, and he should know; it's where he worked, after all. When he was not teaching our class of singers, entertainers, Broadway wannabes, and Dolly Parton dreamers about the music business, he was working in it. We listened to him intently, rapt at every word. I blushed at his compliments and choked on my pride when he would use me as a demonstration during his lessons.

I read a quote once by author Jacob Nordby that goes like this: "What an interesting little prison we build from the invisible bricks of other people's opinions." Ah, yes, "other people's opinions." *Propaganda with our name on it.*

Is there anything else in the world to hold such a power over us? Very few things can make us act out, dress up, start a fight, pull a trigger, cause the hurt, or start the war more than our concern over what someone else thinks.

It was two weeks before the semester was over when my teacher addressed the 130 students seated in the stadium room with this:

> Just look out that window. Every one of you wants to make it onto that street right there, don't you? But I have heard every one of you sing and very few of you even have a chance to make it in this town... with the exception of one: Melissa Radke. She is the only person in this class who has a shot, but unfortunately, no one will ever give her the time of day because of the way she looks. Look at her! No one is going to want to listen to one note out of her mouth.

I have shared this story different times over the years, and I am always asked the same questions. So, I'll save you the time and trouble:

1. Melissa, do you hate the man for what he said to you?
2. Melissa, aren't you angry at what he said?

First of all, *yeah*, I guess at the time I hated him for saying it, but only because it embarrassed me. I hated him for embarrassing me in front of my friends and my peers. I hated that every eye in the room fell on me and that no one breathed and no one moved. I hated that no one spoke to me on the way out of the room because they were too embarrassed. I hated that he owned that moment in such a devastating way, because it wasn't necessary. There were a thousand examples he could have used; he didn't have to be such a douche and use me. But that isn't what you asked me. You asked me if I hated him for what he said. The answer to that is no. What he said was honest. It was painful and ugly and unfair and mean, but it was honest.

You sound good, Melissa, but "no one buys ugly."

Welcome to Nashville.

"Fine. But aren't you at least *angry* at what he said?" I was never angry at what he said. I was sad. I was disappointed. I wanted to pack my bags and move back to Texas right then in that very second. But I was never angry.

Maybe I should have been, but in retrospect, what I was angry at was that I had been so busy building an interesting little prison for myself with his opinions that I never heard the cell door as it closed behind me. That day, in that moment, he shut out my hope, he took away my freedom. I allowed what *he* thought to become a six-by-eight-foot concrete structure around what *I* thought. I had placed myself at the mercy of his praise. This is a dangerous thing to do.

When our esteem rises and falls on the words *they* use...

When our emotional health is banked on *someone else*...

This is thin ice, my friend. But hey, I get it. I know where you are, and I know how hard it can be. How can we be expected to know who has our best interests at heart when even *we* don't have our best interests at heart? This is the sad truth. He cared very little about what he said, yet I based my worth off of it. He never thought about what he said, yet I obsessed over it.

Looking back, his words were as shallow and superficial as my belief system. Try them on me now, and let's see how far we get. But then? I was aching for someone to hear me, to see me, to believe that I was more than a plus-sized problem. My belief system was so messed up. I shake my head at how quickly I let his words invade the holy place that is my heart.

I swear, if Nashville was a game, I was losing.

But girls like me? When we lose?

We keep tapping. Dancing. Twirling.

STILL NOT ENOUGH

I got in my car and drove.

I told David I was going to try out for a new singing reality show. That wasn't a lie.

I told him that I would be singing "Midnight Train to Georgia." That wasn't a lie.

I told him that I had gotten me a hotel, had taken some cash out of the ATM, and would call him when I pulled into Atlanta. None of that was a lie.

I told him I was fine. *That* was the lie.

I drove for hours. I drove and I cried and I sang and I rehearsed and I sped and I pulled over and I dried my tears and I pulled back onto the road and I drove some more and I cried. I was not okay and I was not happy and I was not going to stop trying and singing and dancing and waving my hands until somebody noticed and somebody gave me a shot. Until somebody looked past what held up my jeans and what fit in my bra and gave me a freaking chance.

There I was, driving to a city I had never set foot in to try out for a show I had never seen by singing a song I had never sung. I had exactly thirty-one dollars in my purse and I was tired.

I waited in line with over a thousand girls, all planning to sing Mariah or Whitney, while three judges sat behind a table wielding enough power to make a person crazy. They hardly ever spoke except to say "Thank yooouuuu." You did not know if you had made it to the next round until you walked off the stage and someone either handed you an invite to round 2 or they never looked up from their clipboard which meant *The exit is to the left, have a nice day, enjoy Atlanta.*

I believe the children are our future . . . *Thank yooouuuu.*
But then a hero comes along . . . *Thank yooouuuu.*

And I-I-I will always love you... *Thank yooouuuu.*
My heart will go on and on... *Thank yooouuuu.*
It had been like this for hours.

I walked to the stage. Eight hundred pairs of eyes were on me, and yet I was fixated only on the three people behind the table. I placed the mic stand in front of me, took a deep breath, and began to sing. When I was done the girls in the room began to clap. The judges had put down their pens and stared at me. The middle judge stood up and walked to the stage. No one in the room moved, least of all me. We didn't know he could walk; it'd been twelve hours and we'd never seen his legs. He walked up, smiled at me, turned to the room, and pointed in my direction:

You wanna be on my show? You better sing like this.
But you better *not*... look like this.
Next!

I walked off the stage and to my car. I closed my door, buckled my seat belt, and pulled out onto the street. I made my way out of downtown Atlanta through glassy eyes. I never stopped for gas or a drink, I never stopped to use the restroom or call my husband. I drove for four hours and never turned on the radio, never rolled down the window, never shed a tear. I went home and crawled into my bed.

I rolled out of it four days later.

I threw my tap shoes against the wall. I was done.

Chapter 12

Water to My Chin.

"*I will not go anywhere.*

  "*I will not go anywhere!*

  "*Do you hear me? I will not go anywhere!*

  "*You cannot send me somewhere!*

  "*You can't . . .*

  "*So, I'm not going.*

  "*I am not going anywhere no matter what you say!*"

David was crying into the phone, whispering to my parents. Yet, I could hear every word he was saying. "The doctor said she needs to go somewhere . . ."

  "*I'm not going!*"

"But she is refusing, and I don't know what to do.

143

No, it's gotten worse. Yes, much worse. Well, she hasn't bathed in a week. Melissa, when was the last time you took a shower or bath?"

"Shut up! Shut up talking to them."

"It's been at least a week, maybe more. She's eating. She's screaming. She's angry all the time. She hasn't been to work. How am I supposed to make her? She won't get out of the bed. No! She just lays in bed twenty-four hours a day..."

"Hang up the phone! Hang it up!"

I grab the closest thing to me that I can throw—a lightbulb sitting on the dresser. I grab it to throw at him, but my anger causes it to snap in my hand. Glass and blood fall to the carpet.

"I have to go. She's cut herself. I don't know...she's bleeding. I have to go!"

He hangs up the phone. I lie on the floor, in the glass, in my blood, and I cry.

It's been this way for months. This fog. This depression. This mental quicksand. That's what it feels like, you know? It feels like I tripped and fell into something that I was totally unaware was even there—and now I'm stuck. I had never heard of quicksand until I was around nine years old. I heard a missionary, who had been living in a foreign country, talk about an encounter he had with quicksand. He explained what it was, what it could do, as young ears and bright eyes watched him from the stage. Jaws dropped, senses heightened. I decided right then and there that quicksand was the scariest thing I had ever heard of and I wanted no part of it. Yet, here I was. Losing to it. Oh, I could move, but only to go lower, slip farther...not to get out. Every day I battled a force I could not reason with and I slipped farther and farther.

On this morning, on this Friday morning, David pulls back the covers and walks me to the car. I arrive at the doctor's office in the same clothes I had put on some two weeks before. I stink, and my hair is oily and stuck to my head. My face is covered with acne. I have put on weight, a lot of weight. I did not have to ask off from work to go to the doctor because I had quit my job. David still thinks I have been calling in sick. Really? For two whole weeks? Sometimes he is naïve. Or maybe he just doesn't want to know the truth. The truth is I quit my job and now my job is to lie in bed until I die or I kill myself, whichever comes first.

Here, in the doctor's office, they run tests on me. They scan me. They ask me questions. They probe me and pinch me and prick me. They ask more questions. They discuss me. They prescribe me. They label me. They send me out of the room. They talk to David. He comes out twenty minutes later. His eyes are swollen. I do not care.

He picks me up from the carpet and takes my clothes off me. He draws a bath and all but pushes me into it. I don't fight him. Only because I have very little fight left. He sits on the side of the tub and checks my hand. Cold water has stopped the bleeding. He looks at my hand and then me; he goes back and forth like this for a while.

"I don't know what else to do for you. They gave me prescriptions that I can have filled, but that isn't what they suggest I do. They think we need to send you somewhere, Melissa. What is going on with you? Where are you? At first you made me sad, but now you're making me angry. This isn't you!" His tears slide down his face and into my bath water. "I'll come down and check on you in a few minutes. Please, baby, at least wash your hair!"

And with that, he turns and leaves the bathroom.

Alone, I sit in the tub . . . water to my chin.

I wish I knew what had happened.

I wish I knew what started the avalanche.

I wish I knew how to fight it or cure it or contain it.

But how do you fight an enemy you can't see?

I sat perfectly still.

(Go under.)

I didn't move a muscle.

(Go under the water.)

This was not my voice. But it was in my head.

(Do everyone a favor and just slip right down.)

I was intrigued.

(No hospitals. No pills. No more watching David cry. No

*more worrying your parents. This is easiest for everyone. Espe-
cially you. If you are looking for a solution, here it is.)*

I did want a solution. I did want a cure.

*(Just go under the water. It's quiet. It's easy. It will be so
simple.)*

Simple sounded good.

*(And everyone—him, · you, everyone—can stop worrying.
Life will be better for everyone. Promise.)*

At first I had been so still, not even the water moved,
but now I lay my head back on the water's surface. Water
began to creep over my eyes, my mouth. I would move
and it would roll off again. The room sat still as my
breathing slowed...even as I write this book, at the ripe
old age of forty-something, I've still never learned how
to breathe underwater without opening my mouth wide
and swallowing my chances...and so, I breathed in my
last clear thought and made plans to sink beneath the
surface. My lungs expanded halfway; a chest full of air
would only prolong the inevitable. My eyes closed and
the walls closed in around me. I would need to take a
deep breath in, in just a moment, but willed myself not
to. The panic set in as my toes began to curl and my
neck began to stiffen. My head bobbed as it longed for
me to make a choice: Let's go ahead and go under or let's
get out. My thoughts grew heavy and the darkness and
panic rose in my head and my lungs. I considered the
cost. I considered my options. I considered the alterna-
tives. I thought about David. With my eyes closed, I saw

my folks. I thought about the children I had yet to have, yet to hold. I wondered about my friends. I wondered if anyone would miss me. I doubted anyone would cry. I thought about my granny; I worried about my pawpaw. I wondered how David would explain it to my cousins, our neighbors, our church.

At the root of it, I was sad. I was sad that I could not ever be what I wanted to be—because I did not look like I needed to look. I was sad that my life looked nothing like I had planned on it looking. That the people who had said, "If you get down, just get back up and dust yourself off," were full of crap, because that didn't work. My attempts were futile, my tries were useless, and my dreams were pointless. I was furious at God. Didn't He know that I had laid out a master plan for my life? Didn't He see how well I had planned and studied and mapped it all out? But none of that seemed to matter. What had the degree been for? What had the vocal lessons been for? Why had I been given a gift I would never have the chance to use? Who does that? Who pulls that mean of a joke on someone? I could not wrap my head around the idea that everything I was created to be was one colossal joke at my expense. I was pitiful and foolish and sad and tired. I was certain that going underneath the water would be the end of the hurting and I was ready to try it because this depression, this illness, this whatever it was, was going to kill me slowly and I refused to let anything else win out over me.

I would make one last decision...even if it killed me.

I heard David moving around upstairs and knew he was nowhere close enough to hear me.

I said goodbye to him in my head.

I said goodbye to my mom.

I sent my love to my dad. And then, without any movement or forethought, without knowing why I was saying it or what it might even be for, I whispered the only other name that had ever meant anything to me...

"Jesus."

I could hear my heartbeat.

"Jesus."

My lips, just above the water, formed the word.

"Jesus."

My eyes filled with tears.

"Jesus."

For the first time in too many months to count, a tear fell down my face.

"Jesus."

I tried to tell him goodbye. I tried to apologize. But all I could say was...

"Jesus."

"Jesus."

"Jesus."

With my toes, I lifted the drain in the bathtub. I lay in the water as it poured down the drain, until it was no more and I began to shake from the chill. I wrapped a towel around me and crawled into my bed. I pulled the covers up over my chattering teeth and I began to cry as loud and as hard as I had, maybe ever. I cried until I fell sound asleep.

I woke up a full day later. I had not tossed. I had not turned. I had no nightmares. David said he hated to wake me because I was sleeping so hard, but it had scared him and he had checked my pulse through the night. When I woke up my face was still broken out and I had not lost weight. My thoughts were not of rainbows and unicorns. I did not hop out of bed with a fresh perspective and a desire to head to the farmers market. None of that mattered. What mattered is that I had woken up at all.

I woke up slowly, cautiously, carefully.

And I dressed.

Chapter 13

Germans Do Bible Studies a Little Differently than, Say, Rednecks.

Here's a little-known fact about me. (Except it's not "little known." Actually, a lot of people know about it—because I talk about it all the time—because I need everyone to know): I hate sitting down with people one-on-one.

I mean, I really hate it. I have never liked it, but now you throw in my rapidly increasing age and my horrifically awkward inability to make small talk and let's just say I would rather have a root canal than drive alone with you to see your new lake house or meet you for coffee to see pictures of your puppy. But, you ask, what do I have against vacation homes or puppies? Nothing!

I'm okay if you let me bring a friend. And it can be anybody! My mom; my granny; my assistant, Erin; or my best friend, Karli, who has had to attend more than one dinner with someone she doesn't even know just so I won't pass out.

Why do I tell you this? Because I need you to know my feelings when I listened to my voicemail messages one day, a few years back.

"Melissa..."

Wait—before I lay out the whole message for you, I also need you to know that the woman calling me was German. Very German. Now, I have nothing against the Germans; they seem to be a lovely people, and thank God for them, because I love sauerkraut. But sometimes their accents make it appear they are yelling at you, even if they are not. Or maybe they are. Most people do indeed yell at me, so perhaps I'm not imagining this. But her accent? It was hard and fast, and I tried to think of someone it sounded like, so I Googled "famous Germans" and the first person that came up was Adolf Hitler. So, yeah, I've made my point.

"Melissa. You signed up to take my Bible study, no? You will begin on Monday. The class will be at my house. Each week. On Monday. Four p.m. See you there. Also. No one else signed up. It will be just you and me. Each week. On Monday. Four p.m. Goodbye."

Scheisse.

———✦

For six weeks, I met with a very tiny German with a very thick accent and a lot of pent-up aggression. Her anger wasn't at me as much as it was at my lack of understanding. We were doing a study on learning about our identity in Christ, and for a daughter from the Bible Belt, who never missed a church service or a choir practice, I knew very little about what God said about me.

Funny, huh? We seem to know exactly what He says about Democrats and Republicans, gun control, and healthcare. But some of us are as dumb as hair about what God has said about us! We know where we stand on every hot-button issue known to man. We just don't know who *we* are. Which seems quite the juxtaposition, to know what we want but not who we are. This is not only sad, but can be dangerous. Just ask the person who enjoyed a bowl of ice cream every night before bed until they found out they were diabetic. The key is not only knowing what we like and what we want. But in also knowing who we are, what we are. Being assured of only one of these things is a real risk to your life.

Each week I sat and listened to one of the wisest women I had ever met as she asked me hard questions about myself—questions I didn't want to answer because I just wasn't sure. I had not been sure of myself for a very long time. I would pour out onto the page how much of a letdown I had been to myself. She would read my words as tears ran down her face. She would often hold me as I cried. She would apologize that the truth of this teaching had not come to me before now. She would sit at her kitchen table, eyes closed, hand on mine, as I read from my journal.

"I think my biggest fear in life is dying with regret. Not the kind of regret like I didn't get to climb Everest, take more vacations, or spend time with my family. My biggest regret would be that I will have spent more days inside the four walls of my house, dying, than I will have spent outside my house, really living. I will regret that mine was a wasted life. I was created for nothing at all. I was a mistake. A factory defect. I will die never having done a thing, or at least never having done one single thing that mattered."

She cupped my face in her hands after I read these words and said to me, "He came so that you, Melissa, might have life and have it to the fullest. Full life. No regret. No defect. We do not worry about the millions of tiny things that need fixing. Right now, *you* matter. So, we fix you."

One of my favorite commercials is called "100 percent Nicole." While listening to the song "Getting to Know You" play in the background, we see Nicole travel the globe to find out she is 46 percent West African and 3 percent Scandinavian and a bunch of other cool stuff from a bunch of other cool places and how we can find out all about our DNA, too, with the help of 23andme.com. I like it almost as much as the one from Ancestry.com about that guy who wore that kilt around all year—only to find out he wasn't Scottish. Truth be told, I may be a little jealous; I don't tend to look into those types of sites much for the little-known fear most Texans have, which is: What if I'm related to my spouse?

But why the rise in that sort of thing, do you think?

Why do you think it is suddenly so important to know where we are from, what we come from, what makes up our DNA, where our families traveled from? Why now?

Because we are lost.

And the only thing a lost person really wants? To be found. But being found is hard. Getting lost is the simple part. Getting lost happens all day, every day. It happens every time we are rejected. It happens every time we try and fail. It happens when we are passed over or scooted around. It happens when we aren't invited, put on the list, saved a seat. We lose a piece of ourselves every single time and before you know it we aren't 100 percent Nicole. We aren't 100 percent anything.

Except tired.

And afraid.

Depressed.

Hopeless.

We are those things. We are those things with a side

of frustrated and broken. And before you know it we are sitting across the table from a tiny, German woman who holds us while we cry and then forces us to try a bite of Baumkuchen.

We are those things until someone looks us in the eye and tells us that we can search the whole world over, we can travel to all fifty states or every single country in the world, track down every ancestor that is living and do the bloodwork to boot, but nothing—absolutely none of that—will heal what has been broken.

It may be interesting.

It might be fun.

It might even be the adventure of a lifetime, but it cannot heal hurt places.

I know that I have a good deal of Irish and Western European in me—it's clearly where I get my temper and my ability to grow facial hair just by thinking about it—but at that season of my life, in that kitchen chair, at that table, with that tiny German powerhouse, I was lifeless.

And no amount of Baumkuchen can fix that.

I spent the next few months of my life with a woman whose last name I still cannot spell. I learned that the Bible is not a fairy-tale book. It is not a book written for perfect people who experience perfect love while the theme song from *Titanic* plays in the background.

Rather, it is a book that includes a running list of His thoughts toward us. It was this book, this encouragement, this learning that allowed me to face several of my fears head-on because why not? What was stopping me? God certainly thought I could. He had always thought I could.

———

I make videos now, on social media. Collectively my videos have been seen over 140 million times at this writing, and with every new video that gains traction I can expect comments like these. Here are a few actual comments that have been posted and seen by hundreds of thousands of people, for your enjoyment:

- "Put down the fork before you make another video, lady."
- "Find a firearm and end yourself."
- "I cannot stand to even look at this lady."
- "I wish I could slap her bratty kids."
- "If I had to climb into bed with that lady I'd better be drunk."

I could go on. But I won't. Because here is what I need you to know.

First of all, I'm fine. I don't say "I'm fine" as if I'm one of those women who say they are fine but secretly cry themselves to sleep. Look me in the eye when I tell you:

I'm fine. I'm not wounded, I'm not shattered, I'm not crushed, and I have lost zero nighttime sleep or cozy afternoon nap sleep from these comments. The things that have been said *for* me are of greater worth than the things that have been said *against* me.

Second, words can harm. They can cut and tear, and we should speak carefully and post cautiously. Our words carry weight. But words like this fly in the face of everything God has ever said about me, everything my husband has whispered to me, and everything my mother has instilled in me. Words like that cannot combat the truth that I have chosen to store up in my insides. Oh, sure, I could choose to carry them around with me, pull them out of my pocket, and obsess over them when the night is long and the road is rocky. But I haven't. These words don't own me. They won't tarnish my name, my confidence, or my skin. Not ever again. The truth I have made a decision to listen to was the game changer against the lies that are sometimes still hurled against me.

And last, on the final day I met with my German spitfire, I gathered up my notebook, my Bible, my purse, and I turned to leave. I got halfway to her door when I turned around to look at her, tears in my eyes, and saw that she was tearing up, too.

"Melissa. I have never met anyone that God loves as much as you."

"I bet you say that to all the girls."

"Every single one of them. And every time it's true."

I hugged her. I thanked her. I walked out her door and heard her say, "*Auf Wiedersehen*, Melissa. I did not think I *konnte hilfe* a redneck, so this was a good news for me."

Silly Germans!

Chapter 14

All Inked Up and No Place to Go.

My mother told me a story when I was younger.

A beautiful fair maiden fell in love with a ghastly creature. She, of course, did not know he was such a dreadful being because whenever he was around her he wore a mask. A mask of sandy blond hair, world-worn eyes, "and a chiseled face...kinda like Brad Pitt." *(My mother's words, not mine.)* To her he was more handsome than any man in the village. But at night, when he would return home, he would remove the mask and become the thing he truly was: an unenviable being that would bay at the moon and frighten anyone who saw him! He had no doubt he would scare off the lovely and fair maiden. She, however, was completely unaware of this side of him. Whenever he was with her he was gallant, chivalrous, charming to say the least; if she only knew it was the mask that he wore, not who he truly was.

As they began spending more time together, the maiden found him to be nothing but kind and soft spoken, gentle and loving. Curiously, he himself found that his former desires to bay at the moon or chase the neighbor children had almost completely vanished. His interests now lay in reading books or watching plays. One night, as you can imagine, he leaned in for a kiss, and it was then that the beautiful woman noticed he wore a mask. He begged her not to remove it—he feared her reaction—but she insisted. She slowly removed the mask to find that the man who "looked like Brad Pitt with the mask on was even more attractive and hand-some with it off; seriously, he looked just like a young Robert Redford." *(Again, her words.)*

"And that, Melissa Paige, is what happens to us when we start acting nice do you hear me because you listen here I don't care if you feel like it or not young lady you are gonna put on a happy mask or I'm gonna put one on for you and I can promise you you do not want that so you can start acting happy and acting like you are having a good time and acting like you are not a spoiled brat and maybe your daddy and I are gonna get lucky and pull that mask off to reveal you have given yourself a whole new attitude adjustment because if you don't we are gonna have a come to Jesus meeting like you have never had before do you hear me?"

I sat for a moment. "Did you just tell me the story of *The Phantom of the Opera?*"

"No, don't be ridiculous."

"I think you did. I think you literally just told me the story of the Broadway musical *The Phantom of the Opera.*"

"*No!* I did not, Melissa Paige. I have no idea whether this monster could sing."

You might be wondering why I shared this story with you. It was so you can be reminded—*as I was, with this story, all the stinkin' time, during my teenage years*—that sometimes what you wear becomes a part of you. Which is fine if you want to look like a young Robert Redford, but it is not fine if you didn't get to choose the mask they put on you.

Ever heard one of these stories? Some are hilarious.

Man goes out.
   Man meets up with friends.
   Man drinks too much.
   Man wakes up with a tattoo of Steve Buscemi on his left butt cheek.

Or...

Woman goes out.

Woman meets up with her girlfriends.

Woman gets a text in the middle of dinner.

Woman is broken up with by her boyfriend of over a year, over text.

Woman drowns her sorrow in queso and tequila.

Woman has a blond friend who can't keep her big mouth closed.

Blond friend says, "Hey, you should get a tattoo, that would be hilarious! Since I'm too chicken to get one, I would feel like I was living vicariously through you. Plus, doesn't he hate tattoos? So that'll show him!"

Woman's other friends say, "Hey, blond friend! Don't do that to her," because they are better people than the blonde.

Woman says, "No, no, no, she's right."

Woman agrees with her blond friend, which was a very poor decision on both her part and the part of the tequila.

Woman wakes up with Barack Obama on her back.

I, for the life of me, cannot figure out why one of those stories was way more descriptive.

Do you have a story like this to share? Of someone you know who now owns a piece of history on their back? Their thigh? Their rib cage? Their forearm? A permanent address to this "great idea" that they once had? I do.

I have a friend who cannot for the life of him remember what possessed him to get the Hindi word for *legislature* on his back, but there it is, in all its glory.

I have other friends who display theirs proudly. And why not? They have been thought out, planned for, drawn out, sketched, and resketched. They are beautiful, like works of art down the side of their upper arm; what they have chosen *means something*. There is a story behind almost every drop of ink.

I'm the former.

I woke up one day with tattoos across my . . . *everywhere*. Not literal ones, of course—I'm far too big of a chicken for that. In fact, the only tattoo I ever wanted was of David's name on my ring finger. I went in and asked about it once, but the guy looked at my hands and said, "Are you sure? It tends to spread on this kind of skin." I have no idea what that even means, but I decided it wasn't for me. I have an entire Pinterest page dedicated to ones I like, should I ever grow any sort of threshold for pain, but I'm not holding my breath for that to happen. I prefer to be like the blonde in the story earlier in the chapter who persuades her emotionally devastated friend to make a life-altering decision at the least opportune time. I mean, I don't know who that girl was in that story, but she sounds like a great time. *Am I right?*

I don't mean I woke up one day with Dorothy, Rose, and Blanche on my ankle (although that would be *awesome*). I mean that I looked in the mirror one day and barely recognized myself. I wasn't even me anymore. There, on every inch and across every scar, around every sun spot and in the crease of every wrinkle, were words others had left on my skin. If you looked close enough, if you squinted your eyes and looked for a long while, you could find me, there, amid the markings. I was a shadow of who I used to be. Long gone was the girl with guts, the storyteller and the clown, the friend and the daughter. I was a mark-up of everything they had said about me. I wore their hatred and their hurt, their disdain and disrespect. For someone who is deathly afraid of needles, I sure am quick to lie still while someone etches their judgment on my frame.

Godhelpusallifmymotherwasright. Maybe what we wear *is* what we become.

Right, wrong, or indifferent.

Look at any Sunday in November and you'll see fifty thousand people who think they are a Dallas Cowboy, a Chicago Bear, or Tom Brady. Of course, they're not, they just paid $120 to pretend like it! But for that game, for that moment, for that afternoon, we are invested. Gone are the armchair quarterbacks. We are playing to win. Don't believe it? Look at the name on the back of their jersey. Hey, I'm not pointing fingers! Why else do you think I wore that cheerleading skirt for eight of the most formative years of my life? (See "Cheerleaders: Part 1"— or don't. Whatevs.) Because if we wear it long enough— we just might become it.

I have a story to tell you about this. I know you're shocked.

My senior year of high school, our church youth group visited a large water park about five hours from home. It was a fun, hot summer day filled with my friends and my first taste of mint chocolate chip ice cream. I wore a Los Angeles Lakers T-shirt over my bathing suit, which should come as a surprise to no one. (Did you think I was a Lakers fan? No. I'm a shirt-over-my-bathing-suit fan.) There were lifeguards all over the park, seemingly at every turn—and one really cute one noticed my shirt. "Nice shirt. You like the Lakers?" he asked, as he grabbed my inner tube and pushed me down a raging rapid. *(Playing hard to get at a waterslide? Genius.)* Considering there was no way I could answer him when I was going down a waterslide, I made my friends ride that same ride with me another four times. I was able to tell him that yes, I did love the Lakers. *(Ask me if I can give you the name of one single Laker in the nineties. Go ahead, ask me. Did Kobe play in the nineties? You know what? Don't ask me.)* On my last ride down, he asked me for my shirt and we did this flirty exchange where I would give him my Lakers tee if he would give me his lifeguard tee. Now, I feel like a certain amount of training comes with wearing a lifeguard shirt, whereas absolutely no sense at all came with wearing that Lakers tee, but nevertheless we switched, and in that moment I became an honorary lifeguard. That's right, me. A woman who, at the age of forty-three, still cannot go underwater without physically holding her nose, was given the power to breathe life back into lifeless bodies. Until three hours later, when a woman swallowed about ten gallons of water at the end of a water coaster and started throwing up. While this seemingly kind German family who wanted nothing more than to save their *mutter* yelled, "*Rettungschwimmer! Hilfe!* Lifeguard! Lifeguard!" I walked past them like my feet were on fire. Suddenly I heard, "There's one! There's a lifeguard!" I put my head down and kept moving. You had never seen anyone remove a shirt so fast in your whole life. "You really shouldn't wear something that you're not!" I could still hear onlookers yelling at me as I hung my head and ran away. Which felt like such a slap in the face since I had gotten after several people earlier in the day because *"There can be no running in the water park!"*

I think I've made my point.

Be careful what you put on. You might find it fits... until it doesn't.

There is a good chance that even now, as you read this book, you are wearing the tattoos of a past you no longer want to live. But those words are painted on you. Engraved into your skin. Your ex called you *psychotic* and you believed him. That word stung, and it held on... it's still holding on.

You were called a *bitch*. But are you? Is that how you

acted when you were angry, or is it really who you are? I bet it isn't. I bet you were simply called that, and now you are stuck with it, because you let it in. You let it soak into your skin, and it won't wash away.

You slept with a married man and you've been a *whore* ever since. Never mind that it was a lifetime ago. Never mind that you are married with a family now. You cannot outrun what is forged across your skin and across your heart.

You overheard them talking in the bathroom and they were right, you were a *slut*. But that was one time. One time that you can't get past and you can't get over. One time you wish you could erase but you can't... just like that word they called you, you can't erase that, either.

What else have we been called? What else have we been labeled?

Want me to go first? Okay... they called me:

- Fat
- Ugly
- Lazy
- Embarrassing
- Dreamer
- Talentless
- Gross
- Sweaty
- Smelly

- Waste of time
- Cow
- Dyke

And I wore these things around on my skin for a large majority of my life. I was no more *lazy* than I was a *lifeguard*. Both were lies, and yet both were branded across my body. What about you? Do some of these seem familiar?

- Pig
- Easy
- Ho
- Slob
- Skank
- Trash
- Snob
- Boring
- Dumb
- Dirt
- Useless
- Worthless
- Lost cause
- Nothing

I could go on, but I don't want to. It's enough. It's been long enough. You've worn them around like tattoos you never wanted, stains you never asked for. They are embedded in your skin and in your life. They chart the course of everything you do and every decision you make.

They determine whom you live with and love, how you parent, and what career you have—or don't have. They are responsible for you believing you could get that promotion—or not. That you were worth the love—or not.

They have been with you for so long now you do not know if they are your friend or your enemy. Hear me on this: They are your enemy. They are not art across your back; they do not tell the story you are wanting to tell. They are lies from small people with big voices. Don't let cowards with lung capacity ever again determine your value and your worth.

Tattoos can be removed, you know? It's no walk in the park, but it can be done. It's time consuming, and it's not cheap. Not to mention everyone I've ever asked has said, "Heck yes, it hurts!" But I figure it's small potatoes when compared with how bad it hurt getting them.

When your stepfather looked at you and told you that you were "dirt, less than dirt," I'm guessing that hurt worse.

When your friends ran away because your reputation might cast a shadow on them.

When those lies were told and those stories were created, with you as the leading lady. Did that hurt?

When you stood on the stage...

When you entered the room...

When you walked to the front...

When you stepped up to the mic...

When you were lied about...made fun of...denied... ignored.

Trust me, those times hurt worse than the discomfort of removal.

The removal process is just that: a process. The very definition of process is "a series of actions or steps taken in order to achieve a particular end." If you are going to fully remove the markings of your past, you should plan on it requiring several different steps or actions. That's okay—anything worth doing is worth doing a *buttload* of times. As much as I would love to tell you that I just woke up one morning and decided to erase these tattoos from my skin and never look back, I would be lying. More than once I found myself going back to the very words that had left me damaged. Some days it's just easier to believe you're worth nothing than it is to believe you're worth everything.

But still, I persisted.

For every word, there was a better word.

For every lie, there was a truth.

I replaced every negative with a positive.

I never stopped.

I never will.

I cannot afford to believe those lies one more second of one more day. They don't mark me anymore, and they certainly do not own me.

I spoke differently to myself. I cared for myself more tenderly than I ever had before. I searched out truth and found it. When the tide rolled in and the fog surrounded me, I clung to the words I had found written about me. Slowly but surely, these words brought life to my aching bones and created art out of devastation. For every word meant to destroy me, these words I read brought life to me:

- Beautiful
- Saint
- Adored
- Redeemed
- Forgiven
- Loved
- Sought-after
- Pursued
- Child
- Wanted
- Great
- Peace
- Truthful
- Established
- Strengthened
- Sane

Time after time after time, I repeated the process. When my thoughts told me I was disgusting, I reminded them I was desired. When I felt like a loser, I reminded myself I was loved. It was not easy, and it took some time, but I wasn't going to be inked up by idiots anymore. One day I just decided that *I* would choose what words I would hear and *I* would choose what words I would keep and *I* would choose what words I would allow to penetrate my skin.

I don't know if my mom was telling me the story of *The Phantom of the Opera* or not. I went on a choir field trip to see it in the ninth grade, but I fell sound asleep and have no idea how it even ends. I do know, however, that she was right. Exchange the scars of the wounded for the rally cry of the overcomer and before long, you *are* an overcomer. Not because it's magic and definitely not because it's easy, but because it's possible.

Replace *lost* with *rescued*.

Transform *forgotten* into *forgiven*.

"Aren't we supposed to be ourselves, Melissa? Accept who we are?"

No, not at the risk that you become less than you were ever supposed to be. You've been playing a character that you were never intended to play. Someone told you what you were, but, *oh my love*, how do they know this? They didn't create you. They didn't put inside you the tender working of magic that makes you, *you*.

The role designed for you was always bigger than the one the critics crowned you with.

It was always more stunning and exciting and delicious.

You just listened to really small people with really small . . . *roles.*

But do you hear that? They are striking up the orchestra now, just for you. It's time for the next act, and you have the leading role. You are not what they said you were. So, walk out on the stage and take back what was always yours.

Chapter 15

My Dad Looks Nothing Like Denzel.

Hi, Dad.

Hi, baby! I was just thinking about you. How are you doing?

I'm fine. Why were you thinking about me? What are y'all doing?

I'm just about to take Mom to see you-know-who.

Oh, that's right, the Denzel movie came out today!

Yep. I sure wish you were here to go with us. I was just telling Mom that; I guess that's why I was thinking about you.

I wish I was going to see it, too. Are you on your way out the door? I can call you back.

Nope, not yet. She's still putting on her shoes—which means she has to bend over—so you know we got about ten minutes. How was your day today?

I'm telling her you said that. It was fine, I guess. Nothing special. It's pretty weather here today, though.

Yes, Tennessee has beautiful weather, unlike here where it's 103 degrees in the shade and we are being swarmed with love bugs right now. Is David at the restaurant tonight?

Gross! Oh, I hate those things! Yep, he's picked up extra shifts because we "need the money" so I'm just hanging out here.

You just did air quotes around "need the money," didn't you? You know, needing money is a very real thing—especially for the man paying the bills, so don't knock it.

I know, I know...but we are always on a budget. Oh, my word. I don't ever want to hear that word again!

Yeah, really, this must be like the third time you've ever heard in it your life.

Are you kidding me? If I ever meet Dave Ramsey personally I'm going to punch him in his nose.

Is that why you're sitting home tonight? Your friends aren't doing anything? It's a Friday!

I know, but it was either that or keeping the lights on, so I told them to go on without me.

What are they doing?

They are meeting up at Kelli's house and going to eat Las Palmas on the patio and then to a movie.

Denzel?

Yes. Of course. Don't make me cry, Dad.

You know your mother must be at opening night of anything Denzel does; that was written in our marriage vows.

Well then, I guess I get it from her!

I thought that was your rule for all things Sandra Bullock?

Her too! Trust me, if she ever has a movie *with* Denzel, then I'll probably need to take a personal day.

Hey, baby, would you do me a favor?

Yes, sir.

Would you mind going up to the guest room upstairs? The last time your mom and I came and visited I think I left something up there. Can you go check?

Okay, I'm headed upstairs...

Don't hurt yourself...

Shut it. Okay, I'm in here.

Do you see that candle holder in the corner of the room, on that shelf?

Yes...

Go over to it and pick up the candle that's inside it. Tell me if there's anything underneath the candle.

Why in the world am I looking in a candle holder that I didn't even know I... Dad! What in the world?

Go out tonight and have fun with your friends.

Dad! Seriously! It's a hundred-dollar bill.

I know what it is. I left it there.

But why?

Because I love you.

Seriously, Dad. Why is this here?

Because I knew there might come a time when you'd need a little help and I wouldn't be there to give it to you.

Dad. (I start to cry.)

What?

You don't know how bad I needed this.

Sure, I do.

I'm not kidding, this is the nicest thing . . .

That's what dads are for.

I just feel so . . .

So, what?

Guilty.

Why?

Because we're so poooooooooor! (I'm crying harder.)

That's nothing to feel guilty for! Poor is how you feel; it's not who you are. You are loved, Melissa Paige. I love you so much that I'd get in my car and drive to Nashville right now just to hand you that money if I didn't think your mom would kill me. But she would. So, listen to me . . .

(I continue to cry.)

Melissa . . . listen to me . . . I can't be with you, so I left things that I think you'll need all over the place. Don't go snooping and looking for them. I assure you that I will let you know where they are at the exact time you need them. Plus, I'm too smart for you. You'll never find them.

What if you forget where they are?

I made a list so I won't forget. Besides, the candle holder was the easiest. The others are way harder.

So, whenever I need something, I just have to call you?

Yes. I've already placed everything you need right there inside that house. It won't solve all your problems, and I'll expect you to do your part and help your husband out with that. But Melissa, this is what dads do.

I don't think all dads do this.

Maybe not all.

I got lucky.

I got lucky.

I love you.

I love you, too. Don't spend that on the electric bill, either. Learn to do that through budgeting—which your husband will help you with—God help the poor man. Go out tonight with your friends. I don't want you sitting home alone. Now, I have to go before I end up telling you what's hidden in the trunk of your car! Bye, babe.

Bye, Dad.

Over the course of my married life I have "uncovered" a new pair of sneakers, an AAA auto membership card, too many gift cards to count, and many, many hundred-dollar bills.

My dad was right. He knew what I would need before I was in need of it—and so he left it here for me to have. When the day was bad and the money was tight, when the pantry was empty and the bills were due, my dad left help in hidden places.

So did yours.

Hidden throughout scripture are His thoughts toward you, and they are not thoughts of love and only love. Though love is, indeed good, it is not all.

He *believes* in you.

He *knows* you.

He *encourages* you.

He is *for* you. His desire is to see you succeed and thrive and live life to the fullest. He created you with innate, unique abilities that belong to you and you alone. He has a vested interest in what brings you joy and fulfillment. He is not some slurred-speech, stumbling-drunk sperm donor who laughs at your attempts and relishes in your disappointments. Whatever it is that makes you perk up, that makes you creative and brave and emboldened and adventurous, well, just believe me when I tell you that He is the biggest cheerleader in your corner and the greatest Father you maybe never had.

He has big plans for you—big, huge, thrilling, exciting. Plans that just might mean you stepping out from behind the curtain or the shadow, from behind the fear and the rejection. Plans that thrust you into a life of fulfillment, meaning, and purpose.

You can sit in the house. You can sit there all night and think about what you could be doing and bemoan the place you find yourself in. Or you could talk to your Father. You could tell Him the situation and watch as He leads you to one treasure—*one gift*—right after another. You could follow His voice to wisdom and hope, to encouragement and direction, hidden treasures that are yours for the taking.

Or you could watch Denzel.

You must admit, both are stellar options.

Just be prepared for one to change your night...and the other to change your life.

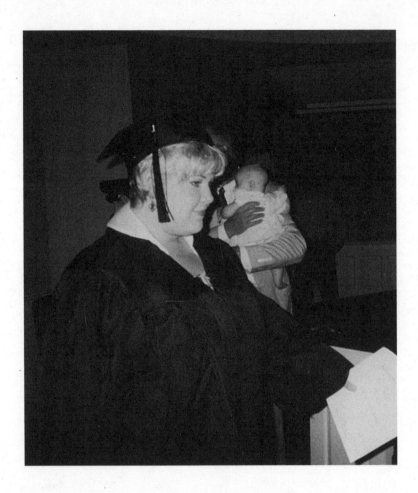

Chapter 16

Cutting Corners. Setting Fires.

He played me the tape.

He rewound it and played it again.

He played it and rewound it and played it and rewound it probably ten times.

"There you are." He'd point to me standing on the back row of the choir. "Oh, but look, now you're gone." He'd hit rewind. "There you are, again...but just wait... now you're gone...there you are...gone...now we see you...now we don't."

Yes, I got it. Message received.

It was the last requirement of our four-year degree. We would sing in the oratorio mass choir and it would be in Latin or German or something equally boring and it would be horrific and the concert would last three hundred hours. We had practiced for it twice a week for months. There wasn't a note we had not gone over backward and forward a million times or more. There were about a hundred of us in the choir, and when it was done we would graduate and I would never, ever sing Latin, on purpose, again.

The night of the concert came. I was getting dressed when a girlfriend called with a much better plan for the evening than spending two hours singing about creation in a foreign language (though I know that sounds hard to believe). The plan entailed meeting up with her and some other friends for dinner. All I had to do was skip the oratorio concert. I thought long and hard about this decision. One was the promise of me getting to use my fake foreign accent for an evening—but the other offered me the promise of a college degree. One was a requirement. But the other was fajitas! Did I make the best decision?

Looking back, no, I'd say that I didn't.

But those fajitas, y'all...

I decided that showing up for the oratorio performance, checking in with the professor's assistant, and then sneaking out was entirely too easy and not nearly showy enough. That is not my style, yo. Instead I would walk in, walk onto the risers with a concert hall full of audience members, take my place *on the top row*, and then, right as the music is about to begin, I would lower my body down, inch my way off the top row, and leave from the back. #gobigorgohome

In order to do this successfully, two things would need to happen:

1. I would need for no one, not any of the audience members, not the dean of the School of Music, not the president of the university, not several local reporters, not the seven or eight professors or the oratorio director himself—all of whom were in attendance that night—to notice my leaving.

2. I would need to be someone other than myself. Someone who did things gracefully. Someone who was not like a Pamplona bull in a china shop. I would need to be someone who could remove herself from *the tallest riser in the room* without falling, being seen, or being heard.

Neither of those things happened.

I left the riser with all the gracefulness of a lumberjack at prom. The choir began to sing and I slowly lowered all five foot eight of me down until I was groin level with a section of tenors. I will admit, it was awkward for a few seconds until I flung myself off the back of the riser, seemingly dislocated a shoulder, and met up with my girlfriends a few blocks away.

Home. Free.

Except that the entire thing had been videotaped. My professor called me into his office bright and early Monday morning. He played me the tape. Over and over and over again. His mouth said that he was disappointed, but his eyes showed amusement, so hope was not totally lost. I would play the card that had gotten me out of trouble so many times before: I would make him laugh. And I did. I made him laugh until he almost cried. But I did not make him change his mind. The dean of the School of Music would decide my fate. On my way out of my professor's office he called my name. I turned around and looked at him. "If there is one person that I have no doubt is going to set this world on fire, it is you. But let this be a lesson you take with you: There are no short-cuts."

I left his office that day and waited for my meeting with the dean.

My meeting with the dean was about five minutes long. She shook my hand and exclaimed that she had heard wonderful things about me and was so happy to finally meet me. She had heard how funny I was and how wonderful an entertainer I was. "And oh, by the way, we have decided that you will not be graduating with your class in three weeks, so you will need to let your family know so that they can make other arrangements if they were planning on coming to the graduation. You may repeat the oratorio experience in the fall and graduate with that class. But truly, such an honor to meet you, Melissa.

I cannot tell you just how many wonderful things I have heard about you. Although, Melissa, I would be remiss if I didn't tell you... your teachers are expecting you to do great and wonderful things—'set the world on fire' were the words they used—but no one gets to do that by cutting corners. The most successful people I've ever met took the long way, my dear. Have a wonderful day."

I left her office in disbelief. How had my perfectly thought-out plan backfired so badly? David and I were going to walk across that stage together. I would not only miss graduating with my friends—*I would miss graduating with my husband!* The worst part of all? I had to call my parents. I had to call my in-laws. I had to let our families know why—when they flew up in a few short weeks—I would not be graduating. I had to let them know that the graduation dinner would only be for one and the cards would only need to be handed to him.

David's parents were very kind and assured me that they would not only fly up for David's graduation, they would fly up again for mine—unless, of course, there was a run on tacos and I felt the need to shirk my responsibilities. Even that was better than my parents' response.

My mother hung up on me.

"There are no shortcuts."

"The most successful people I've ever met took the long way, dear."

"Unless there's a run on tacos..."

I had spent much of my life making decisions off

what sounded the easiest and the most fun, and required the least from me. I was famous for blazing trails *while* cutting corners and skimping on the hard stuff. You wouldn't count on me when it was down to the wire. I was not one to break a sweat, break a nail, or break a date. Well... that had caught up with me. Here I was, in a situation where no begging, no pleading, no promising to give them a shout-out when I won my first Grammy, no making them laugh, no manipulation, and no do-overs would change a thing.

Before my mother hung up the phone I remember my dad, who was also on the call, calmly saying, "All your life you have done the easy thing, Melissa Paige. But easy doesn't pay off; it never has. What pays off is the sticking it out. The staying. The sucking it up and standing on the riser. You made a silly decision at an easy turn, Melissa. But I fear what you might do when the choir concert is over. When the schooling is done and the choices get really hard. When life gets mean. I wonder how long you'll stay on the riser, Melissa. I wonder how long you will stick it out."

I ended up graduating from Belmont University in December 1998. I sat right beside Dolly Parton's niece, which probably means Dolly Parton was staring at me the whole time. *So, WINNING!* I would also like to state for the record that I still do not have a Belmont diploma on my wall, nor did I receive one that night. They would not actually give me one until I paid for my parking tickets. The folder they handed me that night was empty except for the piece of paper that said: *Your diploma is being held in the registrar's office until all payments on overdue parking tickets have been remedied.* That's right, I had outstanding parking tickets from parking illegally. I have been known to park in a professor's spot if it is raining or a fire lane if I'm in a hurry, and once, regrettably, I spent an entire day blocking a wheelchair ramp. Do I feel awful about this? Of course I do, but not enough to pay for it and be a legit college graduate.

See? Something is wrong with me.

So why did I tell you this story? Because maybe you're like me. Maybe you have found that sometimes life asks you to do the heavy lifting and you're not really that into manual labor. *(I know, I feel ya.)* Maybe you have spent your entire life resisting those things that cost more, and I'm not talking monetarily.

They cost you time.

They cost you energy.

They cost you peace.

They may even cost you sanity.

But sometimes, my friend—and believe me, I wouldn't say this if it weren't true—sometimes, the hard work is the only work that can be done. You cannot keep jumping off risers and calling it a night. Sometimes, you have to stay. You have to grow up, wear the dress, and stay for the whole song.

You stay for the grade.

You stay for the love.

You stay for the commitment.

You stay for the payoff.

Is it fun? No.

Is it necessary? Well, that depends: What do you want?

Do you want to spend the rest of your life cutting corners? As Dr. Phil—*that mad genius*—would say, "How's that workin' for you?" Have you found that there is a lot of payoff in running away? I haven't. And that's coming from someone who tried to run for years and years and years. That's coming from someone who got nowhere exceptionally fast.

This season of my life has brought about a lot of public speaking events, and no matter where I go and who I talk to I always bump into this one girl. I should say, this one *type* of girl. She is cute and feisty, well spoken and smart. She has a great head on her shoulders and is highly educated. She has never parked her car up next to a wheelchair ramp and probably never would—but we still have something in common. Want to know what it is? She can't bring herself to do the hard stuff. Lest I jump down her throat as if I'm some professional at facing hard things, I hug her and tell her everything will be okay. But I'm lying to her. I cannot tell you how many times I've walked out of an auditorium or venue regretting that the evening doesn't allow for these types of conversations. Because there was more I needed to say to her.

So, I'll do it here.

After all, this is *my* book, and no one knows this truth more than me. You didn't really think this chapter was just about choral music, did you? You didn't think I'd take an entire chapter to preach to you on the consequence of refusing to sing German? Or Latin? Or whatever it was. No, this was never about ducking out or riser diving. This was about living as an escape artist.

Here is what I wish I would have said to her:

In my life, my marriage, my friendships, and my work, I got going when the going got rough. Don't do that.

Stay on the riser.

I don't care how loud the music is playing and I don't care that you think no one is watching you. *You* are watching you.

Every time you run, know who sees you? You.

Every time you dodge the truth, know who hears it? You.

Every time you deflect the pain, know who feels it? You.

And over time, you have less faith in the person you are, and you grow more suspicious of the person you are becoming. No one became greater by taking the easy way. The greatest leaders and thinkers and innovators, the greatest teachers and truth tellers of our time *all* decided at some point to stay on the riser and keep singing. Do I need to give you the laundry list of great people that stuck it out? Because I can do that. But I'd rather you just understand that at some point all of us have to decide if what we want—and what we want to become— is worth putting the time in. It was a hard truth that I had to come face-to-face with the day I decided that cutting corners had been my MO for entirely too long and had gotten me nowhere. I was in my thirties before I was honest enough with myself to admit that shirking responsibility had taken a toll on me and the person I hoped to become.

So, hear me, *please*. Do the work. Lift the heavy stuff. Say the hard things. Will it require more from you than you want to give? Without question. Will you hurt the next day? Almost certainly. But never trust a doctor who says he can get all the infection out and it won't hurt a bit. Call him a liar and run! No one can go in and re-move the poison without the sting of pain. You've been this way for a long time, my friend. You're a bit broken in places, wounded in areas. Healing can happen only af-ter the hurt has been removed.

But that, my friend, is really back-breaking work; not for the faint of heart is this grueling process. Like finding our way in the woods at night we must move through our pain, standing, crawling, clawing, however we can. Grief expert Stephen Levine writes, "Grief calls us to open our hearts in hell." What a perfect description of this process. Hearts open wide, in *hell*. (Doesn't that just sound amazing? Two tickets, please!) The process of tak-ing the long way, doing the hard work, and cleaning out the infection has never been quick, but we must look at it as if our job—our degree—our grade—our *life*—depends on it. Our job is to walk through hell with our heart open. *Our job.* It's our assignment. It's our task. It's our duty to stand on the freaking riser and hit the high notes.

Hard to believe, isn't it? Hard to believe that the only way to heal your pain is to lean into it, but I learned you can't ignore these things forever. You can plan a great escape—you can make plans to meet up with friends for loud music, drinks on the house, and zero cares—but pain and regret, unforgiveness, and heartache always meet back up with you.

They know where you live.

They have your number.

They aren't going anywhere.

So, do the hard work. Do the *heart work. Do it like it's your job.*

Eventually, I had to come face-to-face with the girl who would rather tuck tail and run than hurt. Who would rather ditch than stay. Who would rather find the nearest exit than face the hard thing.

For the first half of my life, I cut corners in my marriage, my friendships, my jobs, and my spirituality. My motto was: *Look reality in the eye and deny it.*

Until I just couldn't any longer.

Hold a broken marriage in your hand and try to deny it's happening.

Hold a sick child in your hand and see how far running away will get you.

You can't. There you are. Nowhere to run, nowhere to hide.

Sometimes, when it's hard and I want to run, when it's not fun or exciting—I close my eyes and I'm back in the concert hall. It's just me and God. He's cleared the room. The seats are empty now. No one is expecting anything of me. I'm free to run and no one but He will know.

He and I.

Human and Divine.

The risers have been pushed away; no need to sneak, to crawl, to quietly dodge. I can leave at any moment. Only I don't. With Him there I am less afraid. I look the pain in the eye and take it head-on.

With Him there I refuse to live sick anymore.

I refuse to live broken.

I refuse to live infected.

I don't jump off risers anymore. I stay in my place, and I sing.

Through opening numbers and songs in German and fifteen repetitive verses that I cannot even begin to understand, I stay in my place and I sing.

Through seasons of hurt and unforgiveness and betrayal, I stay.

When friendships are hard and it'd be easier to walk away, I stay.

When the doctor's report was the last thing I wanted to hear, I stay.

When I have to choose a casket for a baby, I stay in my place and I sing.

I stay, I stick, I persist, I carry on. I may fall and cry and scream and then get up and sing and spit and claw only to fall down again, but I do it because I want to learn the *freaking lesson*. I want to know what it was all for. I stand on the stage, hand in hand with the one who made me, because sometimes—*sometimes*—the most beautiful melody you've ever heard is the one that begins the moment you make a decision to stop cutting corners and instead, start setting fires.

Chapter 17

Lovers and Leavers.

Moving to Nashville was not the hard part. *Staying* in Nashville was the hard part.

David and I moved on the day of our one-year wedding anniversary. It was 102 degrees outside and we unloaded everything we had out of the world's tiniest U-Haul. We greeted our neighbors next door, five friendly girls with back tattoos and an addiction to Nicorette and Red Bull, and drove to Red Lobster to celebrate our move and our anniversary. We split a meal and ordered waters.

Young, broke newlyweds, unite!

We established ourselves fairly quickly by getting involved in a local church and stepping up to lead a Bible study group that met every couple of weeks in different homes. Our group was full of young couples much like us: broke transplants from other areas who were childless and trying to "make it" in Nashville. This life season still remains one of our all-time favorites. Sure, we'd meet and discuss the Bible and have prayer together, but once all the seriousness was out of the way we'd also play cards, meet up/eat up at Waffle House, and toilet paper one of our houses when someone's sorry attitude called for it. It was awesome!

It was in this group that David and I first met Kylie and her husband, Jeff, who were also transplants from Texas. I don't know if you know this, but when you are from Texas and you meet someone else from Texas, you proceed to embrace them for an uncomfortable amount of time and you feel a bit closer to home. We do not discuss the Alamo or all the things about Sam Houston, which you should know lest you try to stereotype us wrongly. No, we discuss, in precisely this order: (1) How horrible the Mexican food is anywhere else on the planet. (2) How sad it is that no one else is from Texas because it really is the best state in the world. (3) Barbecue. (4) Matthew McConaughey (depending on what his last movie was, of course; this can be a game-time decision). So, to move to Nashville and find that within our own little cluster of friends was this adorable young couple who were also newly married and had just moved from Texas—it was kismet. We were inseparable after that.

Though our husbands got along well and never minded spending an evening together, it was Kylie and I who bonded almost instantly. How did we become such close friends? Over my dermatitis issues. That's right, America! You heard it here: I'm nothing if not a dermatological good time. After David and I arrived late for Bible study one night, Kylie overheard me say I had been late because of a dermatology appointment. She was quick to point out five things I could do for my scalp, and I told her—knowing full well I would never do it— I would call her and get that list. Days later, I actually did. We hung up three hours later. She was one of the funniest, goofiest, sweetest people I had ever met. I was in awe of her, and I fell for her wit and her charm and her friendship very quickly. (My editor said I should add in a cautionary joke here, but I'll leave that up to you the reader: Insert your best cautionary rib tickler here; no doubt there are a million of 'em. Thank you for playing.)

David and I wanted children immediately and were trying desperately to have them, but Jeff and Kylie weren't ready. They were a few years younger than we were and still trying to figure out what it was, exactly, they wanted to do in life. There were nights we played cards so late that they would sleep over at our house. Our weekends became less about missing our families hundreds of miles away and more about taking in the farmers market or miniature golf. We snuck into hotel swimming pools when it got too hot. We snuck into two—

sometimes even three—movies after only paying for one, on rainy Saturdays. Because nothing says, "What is God showing you through this study?" like teaching those under your leadership how to avoid ticket takers at your local theater. It was an awful lot of sneaking on our part. But man, it was a good time. Kylie became a part of everything I did. If it wasn't her tagging along with me, it was me tagging along with her.

We met each other's friends and families.

We grocery shopped together.

She tried to teach me to bake but then gave up and just baked for me. #geniusmoveonmypart

Jeff and Kylie eventually began to lead Bible study with us, and together, the four of us led almost thirty couples every week. We stood beside each other in the church choir and got so tickled that on many occasions one (or both) of us had to leave the stage, which probably grieved God and infuriated the choir leader but only deepened our friendship. We hosted baby showers and girls' nights out for our friends. We planned games for Christmas parties, Easter egg hunts, chili cook-offs, and Valentine's Day dinners. Not to mention the murder mystery party she spent months preparing for but that was a bust when no one could understand the game. We went camping together, stayed in expensive hotels together, and toured Napa Valley together. She made the world's best homemade flour tortillas, which I tried to copy using her recipe, but who wants to eat a twelve-

pound tortilla? So, I think she must have given me the wrong recipe. #geniusmoveonherpart

Kylie wanted a baby for me almost as badly as I wanted one for myself. She and Jeff let our Bible study group know about our roller coaster of a journey to have a family, as well as every lost pregnancy, and she always made sure we were cared for with cards and flowers and a couple of dinners a week. Every pill, every doctor's appointment, every miscarriage, every tear—Kylie was with me the whole way. She was the closest thing to a sister I had. I trusted her with my pain and loss, and she carried those things for me, very *very* well.

Until she didn't.

Jeff and Kylie fought. Often.

She was right—he could be lazy, indecisive, and un-motivated.

He was also right—she was high maintenance, abra-sive, and opinionated.

The truth was, we loved them both and wanted them both to be happy. Yet, after ten years of friendship with them, we could no longer see how that was going to happen. As their marriage weakened and became frayed, the idea of losing what the four of us had—in a town where friendships weren't easily made—grieved us all. They swore things would not change and that we would all continue being friends, but we could quickly see that such a utopian vision wasn't even going to be a possibil-ity. Any time we all spent together was time David and

I spent refereeing. Card nights ended in their screaming matches. What was breaking apart, we could not mend.

It would have been heartbreaking enough had that been the only thing going on in our lives, but it wasn't. David and I experienced our fourth miscarriage during this time. Without sounding like a total cliché: Loss was becoming my only companion. While Kylie was trying desperately to find joy in a joyless marriage, I spent most of my nights crying myself to sleep, and David was in his first year of law school and barely getting by. There were no more farmers market weekends or breaking the law in order to see the latest Bourne movie. No couple's vacations or late-night sleepovers.

We were all adulting... *and adulting sucks.*

I loved David so much. But I'm not sure how "in love" with David I was at that time. Ask anyone who has watched their best friends go through a divorce and they will tell you: Whatever that couple is going through, you also begin to experience, even if it isn't there. I call this the "I-am-going-to-go-buy-a-red-car-and-now-every-car-I-see-is-a-red-car" theory. If they fall out of love, you wonder if you aren't doing so as well. If they argue over money, you do as well. If they say their spouse is a jerk, well, wouldn't you know it? Yours is as well. You begin to view your marriage through a different lens. This is not a good thing.

I began to see David as uncaring and unfeeling.

He didn't care about having a baby near as much as *I* did.

He didn't hurt when I miscarried near as much as *I* did.

He didn't feel the ache and shame of infertility near as much as *I* did.

David could not win for losing.

Never mind that he hung his head in grief at every report we were given.

Never mind that he listened to every fear I had without giving voice to his own.

Never mind that he'd laid his head on the cold metal examination table and cried at our last appointment. All I could see was what was *not* happening to David and what *was* happening to me. I was alone in this. And with every heartache and every D&C and every cramp and every spot of blood, I was in love with him less and less. I spoke to him less and less. I let him touch me less and less.

"You want to crawl in this bed with me and *what*? You have to be joking. I hate you! You're out every night in class or a study group, and I'm here washing your clothes or cleaning your house. I am stuck here! I am stuck in this house and I am stuck in this marriage and I am stuck without the only thing I truly want. I want a baby! Not you! A baby!"

These were the things that I said to him. No, that I *screamed* at him.

In the middle of my broken heart were words so jagged, so destructive, that I ache, today, when I think about them. How I wish that I could take them back. My mouth was going to be the death of us, if he didn't kill me first. I was hard and hateful and every day with me was a battle. But sometimes you find yourself in the middle of a hurricane so severe you cannot take refuge and you cannot give comfort. Enduring one loss was hard; enduring four was grave. It would be a lie to say that David and I were drifting. David and I were broken. It was evident in the separate lives we were living and separate beds we were sleeping in. I grieved in anger and rage; David grieved in silence and withdrawal. Neither of us brought the other comfort; neither of us had hope to give. He was tired of trying and failing. Hearing good news and then bad. Wanting and not getting.

He was giving up.

No doubt I was, too.

Two couples. Two marriages. Two tragedies.

Bodies everywhere.

It was around five forty-five p.m., and if he didn't hurry he would be late getting to class and I would be late meeting Kylie at choir practice. She swore she'd give me her actual tortilla recipe if I didn't stand her up, which we had laughed about on the phone some thirty minutes before. As I ran up the steps to one of the guest rooms, I overheard him on the phone: "I miss you so much. Every woman I see reminds me of you. My break between classes is at nine. Can we talk again then? Okay. I'll call you. I hope I get to see you soon. Oh, crap, I hear her calling me. I gotta go. I'll talk to you a little later tonight. I promise."

My feet slipped and I slid, dead weight, down a few stairs. I sat up where I had landed and sat breathless, motionless. I was perfectly still but the room was spinning. The house was spinning. Everything was moving and I was going nowhere. I could hear the wind. I could hear cars outside. How could I be dead and hear those things?

Everything was moving but I was going nowhere.

That old saying was right: "A woman is like a tea bag. You cannot tell how strong she is until you put her in hot water." And here I was, in over my head. I've given this a lot of thought and I believe there are two distinct types of women in these situations.

Woman number 1 requires no response time; she is 100 percent reaction. She thinks nothing through but instinctively knows what is rightfully hers, and she reacts in accordance. She is strong and fierce and she pities the man who played her for a fool. She can be dangerous. She can be cunning. She can be vengeful. She is alert and sharp and keeps her wits about her at all times. She rarely, if ever, takes any prisoners.

Then there's woman number 2.

I was woman number 2.

There's no description for her because no one ever talks about her.

My very first thought was not "How could he?" My very first thought, which I admit to you sadly and with great vulnerability, was "How will I...?"

How will I get up from here?

How will I approach him?

How will I make my legs work?

How will I get money?

How will I make it home to my momma?

How will I survive this?

My instinct was not to be brave, and it wasn't to stand up and control what would happen in the next ten minutes. My instinct was to tuck tail and hide.

My second thought was that I—*I, I, I, I, I*—must have heard him wrong. That *I* was wrong—not *him*! That my ears were bad or that my judgment was off. That *I* was the problem; *I* was his problem and her problem, and *I* was this thing in the way. This nuisance. This tree everyone had to drive around that had fallen over during the storm.

I wanted to be woman number 1. But I wasn't. I wasn't even close.

I caught my breath and stood; I was shaky, but I will take my credit where I can get it in this story. I finished the climb up the stairs and opened up his office door. Without an opening line, I walked up to him and took his phone. I hit Redial. She answered just as I was praying to God she wouldn't. My very best friend answered the call from my husband's phone with "Hey, that was quick."

I left him. And went to Texas.

(Someone write a country song called "I Left Him and Went to Texas," *stat!*)

Oh, the noise I heard from the peanut gallery...

Leave him. Stay with him. Forgive him. Set him on fire. Tell his parents. Have your dad confront him. Cut him. Talk to him. Forget him. You should move home. You should go back. Sell his car. Key his car. Set his car on fire. And my all-time favorite: You should clean out his bank account, take all his money, and not return his calls.

This person clearly had great faith in us, because I knew the fifty-seven dollars in our account was not going to get me very far.

Three weeks later, I flew back home to David and Tennessee. That was how long it took to decide whether I wanted to stay married to this person. That was how long it took to decide if I could see my future being better with him than what it might be apart from him. I did not—could not—focus on her. I had to place hard things in boxes and file them away in my head and in my heart until a later date, and Kylie was one of those things. This was my marriage, and I had a decision to make. I loved this man with all of my heart, all of my soul. I could not foresee a lifetime without him in it.

But *could I* forgive him?

Would I forgive him?

Those are two very different things, you see: our ability and our willingness.

I *can* mow the yard...doesn't mean I *will*.

David and I began the process of rebuilding a marriage that had, at one time, been very strong, very fun, and very trusting, but that had become very broken, very sad, and very lonely. There was yelling and screaming, storming out, and crawling back. We had been through nothing as a couple up until those last few years and now there we were, bloody and wounded, and looking for reprieve. At times we were a shelter for one another; at times we were less familiar than strangers. We slept together. We slept alone. We were up and down, back and forth, giving up and going forward. We sought professional help, and never once were we shy about needing it. It was hard to accept that every time my body had let me down, so had my heart. In a situation that looked to be one-sided, it most certainly was not. I was a broken and angry woman and had been one for quite some time. We were both responsible for causing what had happened, and if we did not both accept that truth, then we had no hope of salvaging our union.

One year after I walked up those stairs and overheard that call—the call that would change my life and my marriage forever—we were pregnant...again. Elisha Cooper Radke would be born on Christmas Day 2005, and he would stay with us for an hour and thirty-six minutes. He looked just like me, but was tender and mild like his daddy. I would look at David holding him and thank God that I fought for what was mine, fought to heal what was broken. We would kiss our boy goodbye only moments after we kissed him hello. We had never known a grief quite like the one we experienced that Christmas Day, nor had we ever known such a joy.

The day we left the hospital, David strapped me into the car, placed an empty blanket into my lap, and began to back the car out of the hospital parking lot. He put the car in park, placed my face in his hands, and looked at me. We would ache together that night and the next day and maybe even forever. But at least it would be together. Without saying one word he put the car in drive and we went home.

It has been twelve years since my best friend fell in love with my husband. Twelve years since he admitted to an "emotional affair," which is no less horrifying than any other type of affair, believe me. It has been twelve years since I lost my best friend, since I last had lunch with her or laughed over the phone with her. I have had twelve years to grieve a friendship that had to die. Let me tell you about a twelve-year view: It can give you a lot of perspective.

A few months after I had left Texas and come home to David, when we were neck-deep in counseling, I prayed this prayer one day in my car: "God, I want to tell people. Okay. Fine. That's a lie. I want to tell *everyone*; everyone

I know and see and everyone who knows her. I want to make sure people know her for what she is. What she did! I already feel them whispering behind our backs; why can't I just tell them? Why can't I clear my name? See how good of a prayer this is? I just want to be able to tell the truth no matter how much it rips apart someone's name and life. Amen."

(Are you reading this book to learn from my maturity? That was a mistake on your part. No refunds given.)

Suddenly, and without question, I got my answer.

(Which goes to show you that prayers—even in the craziest of ways—are still answered. Like, this one time I was praying that God would please change David's mind and let us get a dog and that I would promise to take care of it and feed it and walk it and then right that very minute I hit a dog with my car and cried myself to sleep for two weeks. We got a cat. Then, another time, I was praying that God would strike David dead for getting on me for texting while driving and then bam! Right that very minute I hit a stop sign. So, see? God has His ways.)

I knew, suddenly and without question, that I should not speak about it for ten years. Ten years! *Y'all!* I had to shut my mouth for *ten years*. No talking, no slandering, no running anybody out of town like it was the Old West. I had to sit back, take notes, and keep my mouth shut. Apparently, God knew a ten-year perspective would be better than say, a ten-week perspective. He's smart like that.

May I tell you what I learned in those ten years?

For starters, never had anyone wounded me like Kylie wounded me. It was one thing to forgive David (I was paying eighty dollars an hour to learn how to do that), but Kylie was different.

It made no sense to me. It was *me*! We were friends. *Best friends.*

How do you do that to another woman?

A woman you love?

What about *girl power* and *girls rule*?

Not to mention, we are supposed to *run this motha . . .* Beyoncé said so!

How do you hurt someone who has shared every secret with you? How do you play to the very weaknesses they've told you about in confidence?

My mind raced with revenge and I was fixated on ways I might could hurt her right back. I was consumed with anger, venom, and poison. The madder I got, the un-healthier I got. I was losing sleep at night, spending hours of my day hating her. My unforgiveness was killing me. So, like anyone who has no idea what to do—I went online, straight to Amazon.com. I typed in "forgiveness" and was greeted with 2,108 different options. I scrolled down until one word jumped out at me: *total*.

The book was *Total Forgiveness* by R. T. Kendall. I had never heard of the book, had no clue who the author was, and had no inkling if the book was any good. I did not know of one person who had ever read it. I simply ordered it because of the title. (Kind of like you did because you saw the word *cake*—don't lie.)

Because of that word. *Total.*

- Not a little bit.
- Not sorta.
- Not only on good days.
- Not only on strong days.
- Not on days when my marriage was up.
- Not on days when I thought I looked good.
- Not only when I heard her name.
- Not only when I passed her car.
- But totally.

Doing anything "totally" is freakin' hard.

The book arrived at my house three days later because sometimes young couples can't afford Prime, okay? Okay. I opened the brown box it came in and held it in my hands, unsure if I wanted to hand over my hurt. Sometimes the things that hurt us the most fit so well in our hands that we aren't sure we should release them. That's a beautiful trick, though: It never really fit in our hands; we've just held on to it for so long we aren't sure what we'd be without it. I flipped through the book until I landed back in the beginning, on the author's dedication page. It was a small dedication to his daughter—only two words, in fact. A book on forgiveness had come to my door and in it were two life-affirming words: *For Melissa.*

I read every page.

Now, here's where that perspective comes in, because here's what I learned in those ten years. Kylie didn't hate me. In fact, I believe, at one time, she loved me very much. But she also wronged me. I say this with an absurd amount of confidence, but I don't for a second believe that she became my friend so that eleven years later she could swoop in and steal my husband. In fact, I think she's sorry for what transpired. I think she was in an unhappy marriage and I think she was a very broken person. I also think that the genius who said, "hurt people, hurt people" was right. Heck, I was living proof of that.

So, I forgave her. Totally.

I also forgave David. Totally.

Forgiving him has paid off for *us*.

Forgiving her has paid off for *me*.

As far as David goes, well, at the time of this writing we are in the twenty-third year of a very human, very wonderful marriage. I know, now, what pain looks like when David wears it on his face. I know that when his heart breaks he retreats, so I no longer let him run from me. (He knows that when my heart breaks I become a real pain in the...)

I don't let him avoid feeling pain by filling up the space with conference calls, work weekends, or podcasts. He doesn't let me avoid pain by pretending we are roommates and not lovers.

If we are going to fail—we are going to fail together.

If we are going to hurt—we are not going to hurt alone.

If we are going to love—we are going to love each other...for another twenty-three years...or until Channing Tatum sees me across a crowded Chick-fil-A.

It's a vulnerable thing to write a story like this. It's a hard thing to admit that one time, twelve years ago, you sat on the stairs broken and afraid of your own voice. It's embarrassing to admit you weren't strong enough to be woman number 1, but you were cowardly enough to be woman number 2. History applauds the hell-raisers and the heroines; we build statues to spitfires and read about the radicals. Not one time has anyone ever decided to forgo the chapter on Joan of Arc: The Image of Female Heroism in order to read Melissa Radke: The Biggest Tit.

That's okay. I am part of a different type of hero. Oh sure, it would have been nice to have been born kickin' butt and takin' names, slinging guns and blazing trails. But I am quite fine being part of a special group whose motto is "I once was blind, but now I see."

I'm sorry my words destroyed you; they destroyed me, too.

I can see that you are hurting; I am hurting, too.

We are losing...and this isn't something I'm willing to lose.

I am fine with the view that perspective can bring you.

The beauty that forgiveness will grant you.

And the marriage that perseverance will serve you.

Let no one ever mock the woman who stayed. Who buckled down and braved through. The fight wasn't easy—but the marriage was worth it.

The love was worth it.

The man was worth it.

Who cares that you lost your breath at the point of impact, that you tumbled down the stairs and landed in heartache. What matters is that you stood up, wiped yourself off, and did the hard work. The *heart* work. They say you aren't strong because you stayed? I say you're Hercules because you did.

In fact, I say, every good love story needs a hero like you.

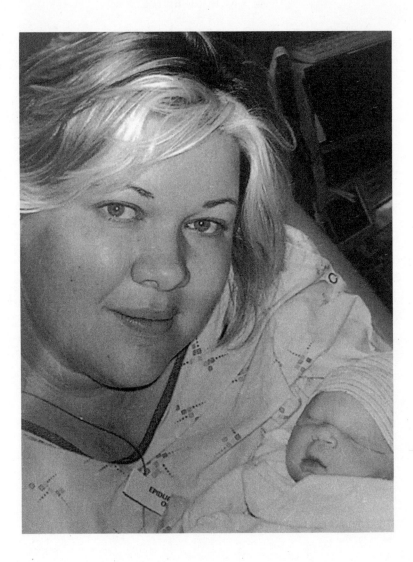

Chapter 18

Everybody's Doing It. Want Me to Do It for You?

They looked so happy. They looked adorable and well dressed, very matchy-matchy, in fact, which was a surprise because normally that was not David's thing. I once tried to get him to wear a RADKE VACATION 1998 T-shirt with me, and he laughed until he fell asleep. But there they stood, on the sidewalk outside of our church, him in a suit, her in a yellow dress, holding hands. Their children matched them in both color and spirit: Their daughter had on a white Easter hat and their son was in khakis. I knew instantly his daddy had picked out those pants.

I sat in the parking lot, inside my car, with the air-conditioner blowing full force on my face, trying to dry my tears. I couldn't get out, couldn't let them see me. If every game had a winner and a loser, guess which one I was? I could envision the embarrassment I would feel from getting out of this car. I would have to walk past them. Him, David, the love of my life and her, one of my dearest friends. I couldn't do it. It would be too awkward. For me and for them. My arms empty, theirs overflowing. My heart broken, theirs whole and beating soundly. They stood there, a model family, him shaking hands and her hugging necks as people walked in and out of the church. The kids played and jumped, and garnered attention, as kids do, and the adults laughed and acted exasperated, but they weren't: This was what family looked like. This is what young parents looked like. It was what I wanted to look like. With him. I loved him still, my damaged heart, my sick stomach, and my dry throat told me as much.

I put my car in reverse and slowly backed out of my spot. I looked in my rearview mirror for children playing too close to cars, or former friends too embarrassed to say hello. I saw both. As I drove slowly away I looked to my left once more—because like a dog that returns to his vomit, we sometimes can't turn away from what could have been us, what should have been us—and he spotted me. David stared at me inside my car. I was almost sure he looked at me like he missed me, but his son grabbed his pants leg and soon his attention was diverted. Without a wave or a whisper, he took his new wife's hand and the four of them began to move to their car. I couldn't stop my tears now. They fell long and hard as my heart broke in two, again and again and again until...

I woke up.

Another night, another dream. The dream was always the same; the only difference was who played the part of David's wife. Some nights it was my closest girlfriends; some nights it was a stranger—and I am not entirely sure which was worse. But no matter the woman, the message was always the same: She can give him what you cannot.

Morning after morning, I would wake up having watched a movie of what could be his—if only I would get out of the way. Then he could find her, love her, have kids with her. Would it hurt me? Yes. But in those dreams I saw how genuinely happy he was with someone who wasn't me. How happy he was with kids. He wanted those children, and if he had to replace me to get them, well, maybe that was best. I knew I was letting him down, and there was nothing I could do about it.

Infertility is a wonderful thing, isn't it? (*If you're looking for the biggest lie in this book, here it is.*)

Infertile. No one even uses that word anymore.

Barren. What is this, Rome B.C.?

You don't go out to tea with your girlfriends and spend a lot of time throwing around words like *infertile* or *barren*. Why? Because they're buzzkills, man. You might as well throw out *cannibalism* or *Dow Jones* while

223

you're snacking on scones. Are you kidding me? Talk about bringing a room down.

Yet I could walk into my OB-GYN's office and my file—which was as thick as my thighs—seemed to have those words plastered all over it. Here is an especially favorite moment: the inevitable trip to a specialist's office. Oh, how I hated walking in and seeing that my file had made it there two days before me. So why, when the doctor finally came into my room, would he open that file as if he had not seen a word of it up until that moment? Really? You put no prep time at all into my visit? For God's sake, I *douched* before I came to see you, and you haven't even bothered opening up to page 1?

"All right, little lady, just hop on up the table here for me, if you would."

And then I would hop up on a table where I would spread my legs for doctor number 7. I always wondered why I never dated much in high school or college and now I realized it was because God knew I would go through a season where I would have to open my legs up to every man I saw in a white coat. I once saw a butcher putting out the steaks at the grocery, and if David hadn't stopped me I would have dropped to the tile floor and spread my legs apart while saying my go-to line: "So, seen any good movies lately?"

But this was where I found myself. On a cold, sterile table, while a man I had never met asked me questions I was sick of answering.

How many times have you been pregnant?

Five.

How many children do you have?

None.

How long between each pregnancy?

Around two to three years.

So you have trouble getting pregnant?

Ummmm, yes.

And what methods to conceive have you tried?

It's probably all written down in the...

I mean, have you used pills? Shots?

Ohhhhh...is that what you meant?

(You can roll your eyes while lying on this table; go ahead, they won't even notice.) I have used thermometers and calendars and pills and shots. I have had a surgery and another surgery. I have doubled up on said pills and said shots. I have tried yoga and holding my feet up on a wall for twenty minutes after having sex. I have tried diets and oils and specialty vitamins. I have tried placing an entire stack of pillows under my butt while having sex. We have done it on rainy days and sunny days, hot days and cold days, early morning and late at night. We've done it when we wanted to and when we didn't want to. We have had sex while laughing and lots of times while crying. And sometimes, because it is far more like a science project than a moment of passion, we have done it while saying absolutely nothing at all. We went to the beach and to the lake and to a cabin in the woods. We have had sperm washed, sperm injected, sperm tested. We have had me diagnosed, rediagnosed and re-rediagnosed. We have given up alcohol, fatty foods, and reality TV. We have prayed before sex, during sex, and after sex. And yet, here I am. Zero babies.

So, you have tried pills?

Um, yeah, we have.

And this was how it went for me, for twelve long years, this was exactly how it went. They would poke and prod and make small talk while they gathered their thoughts and wrote in my chart, only to tell me my situation was "unexplained." Do you know what unexplained infertility should actually be called? It should be called "We got nothing for that." Imagine how much thinner my chart would be if inside of it they just wrote "Per Melissa Radke infertility study: We got nothing for that. Good luck and good night." Unexplained infertility means that there is no logical reason why zero percent of this stuff is working, and it seems, Melissa, that you can only get pregnant when the temperature is at a balmy seventy-two degrees with a slight northerly wind coming in from the coast, the stars are aligned, and McDonald's is having their famous Monopoly game going on at all participating locations.

So see? I could get pregnant; it was just really, incredibly, unbelievably hard.

Sadly, it wasn't just the getting pregnant that was the

problem—it was the staying pregnant. ("You see, you know how to *take* the reservation, you just don't know how to *hold* the reservation. And that's really the most important part of the reservation, *the holding*. Anybody can just *take* them." That *Seinfeld* quote perfectly sums up my barrenness.) As difficult as the getting pregnant was, I also couldn't stay pregnant, and really, that's the most important part of the getting pregnant—the staying that way.

During my twelve exciting years of "we got nothing for that," David and I were the Sunday school teachers of the largest class in our church, the one for young married couples. Pop quiz: Do you know what young married couples do a lot? You got it! Have sex. And do you know what happens to young married couples who have sex a lot? Ding-ding-ding! We have a winner. You answered: get pregnant. And you are correct! Last question, and this one is a bonus question, get it right and that vacation to Toledo is yours: Who is relegated to throwing baby showers for all the pregnant women in the class? If you answered "the Sunday school teacher," then you just won an all-expense-paid trip to Toledo, Ohio, for you and one person you probably don't like very much!

So many baby showers.

I went to So. Many. Baby showers.

Made so many of those cucumber and cream cheese sandwiches.

Ate so many melted candy bars out of a diaper.

Wrote down "Diaper Genie" in so many baby books.

Oftentimes they didn't know that I was sweating because my second round of Clomid gave me intense sweats or made me drink punch like I was an alcoholic on a binge. They didn't know that I had been inseminated the day before like a head of cattle. Or that I had to leave early because it was time to have sex. At first I hid these things. But the truth is, once you've been pregnant twice and lost the pregnancy twice, people are pretty much onto you. At three times, people are worried about you. At four times, they begin to pity you. At five times, they have lost all interest and are back to asking you to cut the crust off the cucumber sandwiches.

I was no doubt a pleasure to be around during those years. I'm overly dramatic on a Tuesday, but you place three rounds of Clomid—and a heartbreaking amount of loss—in me and you have a gem, I'm sure. I couldn't help any of this. I tried. I tried to laugh and smile and make everyone feel at ease, but I was tired of pretending to not hurt. Pain was getting the best of me. It was creeping into relationships and friendships. It was butting into my job, my home, my marriage. And you add to it that every night I went to sleep I dreamed of my husband falling in love with different friends of mine, friends who could give him what I couldn't. Friends who were prettier than me and were more fit than me. Friends who looked better up next to him, holding their children, holding his hand. I dreaded nighttime, and so my sleep suffered. During the day I was the walking dead, the walking wounded.

Loss will do that to you. It will make you into this thing you had no intention of ever becoming. It will harden you, yet make you soft. It will deaden you, yet make you shockingly on edge. It tears down what you were and replaces it with something strange and foreign. I don't care if the loss is your marriage or your job, your parent or your dreams. Whether loss comes in the form of your joy or your five babies—all named, all wished for, all prayed for, all gone—it leaves in its wake a shell of the person you once were. You can rebuild from loss. Like a fire after the last log has burned to ash, you can rebuild, but you won't look the same or walk the same. The fire might be better and brighter, even. But it will be different nonetheless.

This loss, this inability to reproduce—the way we, as women, are supposed to reproduce—did a number on me. Whatever the worst thing is you can say to yourself, chances are the infertile woman says it to herself when she is unable to do what almost everyone—her son's kindergarten teacher, the nail tech, the hygienist, the sixteen-year-old who hands you your dry cleaning—can do. Your body, the thing that has been with you through it all, for better or for worse, could not be trusted with this simple task. And now you stand completely alone. You cannot count on anyone to help you—not even yourself.

Six months after miscarriage number 4, we found out we were pregnant. Again. To say we were excited is an overstatement, because we were not. We were not excited or expectant; we were not overjoyed or hysterical. We counted the days on the calendar to week 9. Week 9. Oh, the infamous week 9 where we would go for an ultrasound and they would inform us there was no heartbeat. I don't mean to be callous, but callous is all I can give you. That was what that moment had made us. We would go into the ultrasound room, hear the click-click-clicks the ultrasound tech would make on the computer and then the words that we had heard not once—not twice—not three times—*but four times*, "Okay, I'm going to go get the doctor and let him talk to you guys." You don't have to go get him. We know the drill. This is where I get my purse, cry all the way home, refuse to let David touch me for about three months, and then we are back to our little human science experiments. Don't bother the doctor; he's got a lot going on.

Every day I was pregnant was just simply another day inching closer to that doomsday doctor's appointment. But this time around the ultrasound came back different—we heard a heartbeat. We had never heard a heartbeat before, not even once. The heartbeat was strong.

Then news that we had passed the three-month mark. Tell the world!

Then news that the baby was growing right on pace. I've got to call Mom!

Then news that it was a boy. I'll take it in blue!

Then news of a baby shower. *My* baby shower!

Then news that something was wrong.

Then news that "I'm going to get the doctor and let him talk to you guys."

There was news that he wasn't well. News that he wouldn't live. News that we should abort. News that if I delivered I might die.

I decided I was sick of news and I was sick of ultrasounds and I was sick of walking around without a stroller and without a hope. And I was sick of everyone winning at the game I was too inept to play. I was sick that a childhood friend actually called me and offered to have a baby for me. I was sick of loss and losing. I was just *so sick*!

And I said no. I will keep this pregnancy and I will have this baby, and if it means I'm in danger, well, it's no more danger than my emotional state is currently in; both of us could combust at any moment. But I will not abort and I will not listen to you, or you, or you. I've come this far. I'm going to finish this. I'm going to have this baby.

And I did.

I had him on December 25, 2005. I had him at 6:36 a.m. He was beautiful. We held him in our arms while he kicked and screamed and slept and cooed. We held him until the heavens came for him. We did not fight what was happening, we did not shake our fist or clench our teeth. It was still the sweetest and holiest Christmas morning either one of us have ever had.

I looked in the mirror an hour after they had come to claim his body and I saw a face that I had never seen before. For quite possibly the first time in my entire life I thought I looked beautiful. My eyes were swollen almost shut from tears, my face was puffy and swollen from four hours of labor. My hair was a mess and had thinned some from those last few stressful months of pregnancy. But what I saw in the mirror I had not seen before.

I liked what I saw.

I liked who I saw.

I liked her so much.

She had not only withstood the *having*, she had withstood the *giving back*.

I was looking at the strongest person I had ever seen.

And sometimes it takes placing your dreams, wrapped up in a blanket of blue, into the hands of a total stranger, before you can accept that you could have died, but here you stand. It's a sobering thought to think that when everyone was opening presents and hugging family members, you were handing back to God the only thing you had truly ever labored for. What a significant day that Christmas morning was, when a gift was given and a gift returned.

I reached up and touched my face.

I took a picture of that face in my mind.

It is the picture I recall when I feel weak and afraid to do a hard thing.

It is the picture I recall when life says, "You can't," but I know that isn't true because I can...and I have...and I will again.

Dear Miss Danielle.

Hi, Miss Danielle! How are you? I hope it's okay that I am writing to you like this. It's been a while since we heard from you, which is okay. We get it! We know you're busy with nursing school. I hope you're enjoying it and finding it's something you truly love. Are you still engaged or are you married yet? To think of you moving on and being so successful with your life, I just couldn't be happier, or more proud. We were talking about you the other day; like she does sometimes, Remi brought you up and began asking questions about you. I love it when she does that. I love telling her all I know about you and what we talked about when we became friends eleven short years ago. I tell her how you talked a lot when you were nervous and how you loved to watch scary movies. She listens to every word, I can tell. She is holding those things close to her heart.

Last Sunday, as we were getting ready for church, I commented to Remi on how beautiful her hair was. She told me mine was, too, and asked if she got that trait from me. I told her, no, that "Ms. Danielle's hair was some of the prettiest I had ever seen, and you got that from her. Along with your almond eyes and bunny nose." She loves hearing that kind of stuff. Staves off any fear of the unknown, you know? Makes her feel like she knows you, in some small way.

Last weekend Remi played a softball game and pitched for the very first time. Danielle, do you know much about softball? It was scary! Scary for her, scarier for me! Everyone gets real quiet and judgy. As worried as she was that she wouldn't do a good job, I was worried that someone would yell at my kid and I'd end up throwing my pickle at their head. Yes, I'm *that* mom. I doubt you are surprised.

The starting pitcher was getting tired and they

brought in Remi to relieve her. Now—*and this is where things get real*—I'd love to tell you how awesome she is, but I'd be lying. Truth is, she's tiny. She weighs about seventy pounds soaking wet. So, let's just say there's not a lot of speed behind those balls. But I can assure you that what she lacks in size she makes up for in chutzpah. And that's why I'm writing you today.

Danielle, I've never told Remi—or anyone for that matter—what happened the night before you went into the hospital for delivery. Do you remember? Do you remember that I took you to get a pedicure and do you remember what happened? A woman in a pedicure chair a few down from us asked you when you were due and you said the baby was coming tomorrow. She asked you what it was going to be and you said a girl. She asked what you were going to name her and you deferred to me. Politely, graciously, kindly you said, "I'll let her tell you since she's naming her." I have never forgotten what happened next. This woman, this random voice fueled with anger and venom, proceeded to scream at you for the decision you were making. She—in one minute—brought us both to tears.

She testified to her unflinching ability to raise her kids on her own with no one's help.

She praised herself for needing no one.

She revered herself for teaching her kids to do the same.

She trumpeted her grit.

She heralded her pluck.

She screamed at you to "grow up" and "do the same." She mocked my inability to be a mother and having to resort to "buying one." I'm not sure who grabbed whose hand first, me or you. But together we walked out, got into my car. And sat there.

We never said one word about that moment. Not then, not later that evening, not ever. I didn't know what to say. I could see you were hurt and I saw you begin to question if what you were doing was right. I could not sway you, nor did I want to. I needed your decision to be yours, not mine. I have never regretted my not saying anything to you. Besides, what could I have said? What did I know?

I wasn't a parent.

I wasn't a mom.

I wouldn't have known what to say back then.

But I do, now. I know what I want to say to you now. It took me some time but I'm more sure than ever. But first, let's go back to my story...

It was the last inning when Remi's daddy—aka the coach—made his way to the mound (yes, he's one of those dads). She had already struck out one little girl and we needed another one just like that. (I told him to tell her if this was too much pressure we could leave and go try out for the Disney Channel! Right then! Anything but this!) He went and had a few words with her. She smiled, he smiled, and that was that. Later that evening a friend of mine sent me the picture of the two of them, on the mound, hashing it out, at that exact moment. This picture now hangs in our home.

In case you were wondering how the game ended up, she threw two more strikes and 417 more balls. So, we're not holding our breath for any softball scholarships at this point.

Also, I threw my pickle.

I asked him later what he said to her. I'm going to tell you what he said to her, out on that mound, that spring afternoon. I'm telling you because my hope is that were your mind to ever lean toward that nail salon—were it to ever give a moment's credence to that *freakin' idiot*, were your heart to feel heavy— that you will read and reread these words a thousand times.

Read them when you think of her.

Read them when you feel sad.

Read them if you're ever lonely.

Read them if your arms begin to ache and you wince at the void.

Read them knowing that what you did for her

daddy and me remains untouched by any other gift we've ever received (apart from her brother).

"Hi, baby, how you are doing?"

"Terrible."

"Actually, I think you're doing amazing."

"You do? Have you been watching the same game?"

"I have. I've watched every second. I think you're doing great. This is your first time, you know."

"But Daddy, I've had lessons!"

"Oh yeah, that's right. How many have you had again?"

"Six."

"Oh man, only six? Some people have to have lots of lessons before they can even get it over the plate. Are you sure you've only had six?"

"Stop it, Daddy, you know I have."

"But you're getting it over the plate. So how do you explain that? You're doing amazing, Remi."

"Thank you, Dad."

"Also, I'm really proud of you. Because I know you're a little bit nervous..."

"Yes, sir...and I kinda want to go home."

"I know you do. Everybody is looking at you. Counting on you. That's hard! I promise you we will go home right after this. But, Remi, you know what else? You're fierce. You are one of the strongest, bravest girls I've ever known. You know where you get that from?"

(And here's the part you'll love.)

"Miss Danielle?"

"That's right. You absolutely get it from Miss Danielle, and I love that about you. Remi Hope, if you walk every single batter that comes up to the plate, I am still going home with the most confident kiddo on this field, and I could not be prouder. So, don't stop now, baby."

"Okay . . ."

And she didn't stop.

She never does.

Whether she wins or loses, succeeds or fails, the child never stops trying. (Unless a song comes on she really wants to dance to—and then she stops for that.) Remi looks hard things in the face and does them anyway. (So clearly, she has more in common with you than just good hair and a cute nose.)

If I could go back in time to that nail salon, knowing now what I did *not* know then, I would have handled it the very same. As much as it pains me to say that, I would have had to. The choice was always yours to make. As much as I wanted to be, I could not be your knight in shining armor. Looking back now, at your fortitude, I'm not sure you ever needed one.

Danielle, on the day I walked out of your hospital room, with that baby in my arms, I turned to you and promised you that in our home from that moment forward until forever you would be regarded as a hero.

Not because you "did it yourself."

Not because you "didn't need nobody."

Not because you "raised kids to do the same thing."

But because you looked hard in the face and did it anyway. Because I stood outside your door and heard you cry until you could barely breathe but I never saw you waver and I never saw you flinch. I saw you hold a baby in your arms, kiss her, touch her, and do everything you could to memorize her face. Then I saw you hand her off, forever.

I stood there, watching, waiting, counting on you. Like the parents and the fans at that softball game, I held my breath and waited for your next move...and never once did you give in. Miss Danielle, I'm not sure what your childhood looked like or if you ever even played a sport. But if no one ever ran out to the mound, looked you in the eye, and told you how fierce you were, allow me to do it now: You are one of the bravest and strongest women I've ever met, and even if you walk a million more batters, I'm still holding in my arms the most incredible thing you've ever knocked out of the park, and I cannot thank you enough.

Remi was right that day. She did remind us of you. Because when we talk about hard things, we talk about you.

All our love.

Chapter 20

Ode to Big Darla.

Dear Big Darla,

Do you know how you got your name?

I was playing a game called Adult Loaded Questions at a bachelorette party. (I pretty much own these types of parties because of my long list of conquests and salty stories.)

Anyway, one player asked this question: "If you were going to have an adult movie star name, what would it be?" There were various answers that night filled with words such as Glitter, Neon, Limber,

Fancy, and Stiletto. But no one—and I mean, not one person—used the name Big Darla. Except me! I would argue that no one has class anymore. I also stand by that decision and I feel that if I do ever find myself "after years of rejection and failure...spit out of the bottom of the porn industry" (somebody please tell me you got that *Seinfeld* reference) that I would be happy I chose a career name like: Big Darla.

Which is why I gave that name to you.

Because it rocks.

And you rock, Big D.

In fact, you remind me a lot of this girl I knew in middle school. She used to start hair-pulling fights in the middle of the hallway, and she never ever *ever* won. Not once. But she also never ever *ever* gave up. Not once. I'm not entirely sure why everyone was so mad at her, but man, she got in a lot of fisticuffs. And lost. Every. Single. Time. She would just bounce back up pull her shirt back down over her bra, and light up another cigarette. She was so tough. I was scared to look her directly in the eyes.

You're a lot like that girl, Big Darla.

You never stop fighting.

You never stop trying.

When I pull up to really fancy places with really fancy cars, you never hang your head in shame. No! You rattle up next to them and hold your head high. You point to the scars all along your frame and say,

"My kids gave me that one. The dog did that one when we got back from vacation and she got too excited and jumped on me. The missus did this one when she was hell-bent on getting a great parking spot at Rose Nail Salon. And this one was from a renegade firework one crazy Fourth of July..."

All the other cars—with their fancy name plates— look at you in shock. They think you should be appalled at how you look and sound. But not you. You are embarrassed for them, because from where you're sitting, they all look exactly the same. In fact, there are a thousand of them—and only one of you. One after another the sleek cars and the black cars and the expensive cars and the detailed cars roll in. But there is only one Big Darla.

They point at you and ask, "What kind of car are you? No one can even tell anymore." And you reply, "Whatever kind my family needs me to be. If I need to get us out of a ditch, I'm tough. If I need to carry a casserole to a sick friend, I'm careful. And the day they strapped the baby in for the first time, I was the softest ride you could imagine."

They laugh and say, "You couldn't possibly have cost very much." And you answer, "I guess that depends on who you ask. I'm worth more than you think; just ask my family."

They roll their headlights and say, "Show me what's inside. Or are you too embarrassed?"

And you roll down your windows and you open your doors.

You point out the baseball that had rolled up underneath the seat from the tournament you drove the kids to. "We took first place that day," you say, "so I took everyone for sno-cones."

You show them the sprinkles in your carpet from the chocolate donuts your family gets every Sunday morning before church.

The red pen in your leather that to this day says "Remi ROKZ." Because you're hers and it's okay to sign your name on what belongs to you. The numerous amount of empty Chick-fil-A bags really cannot be explained, so you move on from that one.

But the swim towels, the shovel, and the one million grains of sand were all part of a weekend that no one in our family will ever forget.

"You go on their family trips with them?" they ask, perplexed.

"Every time," you answer. "They ask me to go with them, every time."

And you kindly explain how what you look like doesn't matter.

It's what you can hold inside.

And that you know—*from experience*—that you can hold seven children who all have the giggles and two adults who both have splitting headaches, all at the very same time.

You can hold family squabbles and family secrets.

You can hold nerves for the first day of school—and yelps and hollers for the last day.

You can hold memories and emergencies and lots and lots of tears.

And, in a story you would like to soon forget but can't, you can hold three dogs, two cats, and one excruciatingly long trip to the vet.

They back away from you after that, Darla. Do you notice that? It's hard to continue looking at something of great worth when it flies in the face of what we're supposed to deem worthy.

I think that's why I'm so fond of you, Darla. You speak to those of us whose labels wore off long ago; those of us who once were tricked out, souped-up, and fully loaded, but are older now, maybe even slower, and a lifetime away from the showroom floor. *(Don't even get me started on our mileage!)* Maybe at one time, we were all about sleek design and in-dash navigation, but not now.

Now we just want to know the important stuff like:

How much love can you fit inside?

What memories do you hold on to?

Who fills you up?

Who takes care of you?

When you hit the road, who do you hope you're with?

You are an ever-present reminder that what we *were* is not nearly as important as who we *become*. Labels rub off, scrapes happen, and our color begins to fade, but the life we have created inside our four walls is what we carry around with us; it's what sets us apart.

Big Darla, I took this picture of you the other day at my girlfriend's house. That's her car on the right. I'm not sure how much it was but I'm willing to bet the dollar amount was more than you and I could even count up to. You know what she calls her car? She doesn't. It doesn't have a name. I mean, it has a label. But not a name. You, Big D, aren't just scrap and metal to our family. *You are automotive proof that sometimes labels mean nothing and names mean everything.*

Because in the grand scheme of things, after the leather is stained and the lights don't shine as bright, after the color has faded and the tires sag a bit *(can I get an amen?)*, you realize that it was never about how much you cost, but how much you are worth.

Chapter 21

Chicken-Fried Women.

One Thanksgiving, when my family was traveling down in a caravan to spend the holiday with us, I decided to do things a little differently. Forget the turkey! Do away with the ham! On this particular year, my cousin Meridith and I would make the meal and it would be different and fun and delicious and we would sit around afterward to see who went into congestive heart failure first.

It would be: *A Country-Fried Thanksgiving.*

I'm going to give you the menu for that Thanksgiving and it is going to make you feel like you need to go on a jog. That's fine, take a break, jog a lap, start a cleanse, whatevs, just know that it was tasty and delicious and nothing burned—but my house smelled like a grease trap for a good five to seven weeks afterward. So, here's the menu. Are you ready?

- Fried chicken strips
- Homemade mashed potatoes
- Homestyle country gravy
- Fried okra
- Corn casserole
- Broccoli cheese casserole
- Green bean casserole
- Homemade dinner rolls
- Real butter
- Chocolate pie
- Peach cobbler
- Chocolate chip cookies
- Blue Bell ice cream
- Sweet tea

Stop judging me! I laughed in the face of cranberry sauce. I spat on the grave of sweet potatoes. I added bacon to every single casserole we made. And those potatoes may or may not have been made with heavy whipping cream. I regret nothing! We had a great Thanksgiving, and my family still talks about it to this day. Of course, it isn't the food they talk about as much as the body aches we all got once we started on a high dosage statin thanks to our increased cholesterol levels.

Aaaaaahhhh, memories.

Cooking with the women in my family has always been a favorite pastime. Notice I said "*a* favorite." Eating together has always been *the* actual favorite pastime. Many hearts were mended and many apologies were given over my mom's famous chicken salad. A lot of shopping trips and girls' nights were planned over a spread of my aunt Melba's king ranch chicken. Wedding plans and baby showers all came to life with one of my chicken strips in their hands. And whenever we feel like we might be losing too much weight from all the stress we *don't* have in our lives, we have Meridith make mashed potatoes because she doesn't skimp when she adds the cheddar cheese, bacon, and sour cream to them. It's a well-known fact that we hate skimpers.

The kitchen has been the place where we met over the good and the bad, the broken and the hilarious. The kitchen has seen us at our best and our worst, has heard our secrets, and held our trust. Its four walls have surrounded us when we needed protection . . . from the weather, from the hurt, from each other.

Besides cooking and eating, here's what else I have done in the kitchen:

Told my parents we were pregnant.

Played too many domino games to count.

Ran in to find my mom after I was bullied at school, and she put down her mixer and held me.

Made funeral arrangements for my grandfather.

Played cards until the snow let up and the cookie dough ran out.

Heard my parents argue. (And my cousin Brandon heard my parents make up, which was a traumatic moment for him because he was hiding under the table and couldn't come out until they were done. Don't ask him about this. He still suffers.)

We sat in the kitchen to plan our Rosemary Beach vacations.

It's where we heard the OJ verdict, learned the dance moves to "Thriller," and watched a whole lot of Johnny Carson.

The kitchen held all the food after my uncle Donald died, and my aunt Melba stood in the middle of it, alone, and wept.

And it's the room that caught fire when I decided that fried shrimp sounded like a logical afternoon snack for a fourth grader.

I guess you could say that the kitchen might be the room in the house that watched my family members and me grow up the most. I imagine that if you tore it down, removed its boards, and pulled up its floors you would find that they were filled with the things that made us who we are, for better or worse. I wonder what fun a kitchen is without the people you love filling it up. I don't know that I would ever want to find out. So, I sat down, in my momma's kitchen, and talked to the women who have shaped me the most. I will not be sharing all of the interview—mainly because it got into some pretty sexual stuff and some earth-shattering gossip—but I will share some of the pieces that might show you how strong women are made, and how bravery is built up right there within your four walls.

———◄═══

Thank y'all for sitting down with me, today.
Mom: We didn't have a choice.
Melba: We never have a choice. You just tell us what to do and we have to do it.
Mer: Plus, you promised us there would be cookies… and I don't smell any cookies.
Okay, let's focus on the questions I have for you all. I want you all to answer honestly, okay? Remember, I'm recording this.
Mer: No need to worry, guys. She has no clue how to work that phone, so there is no chance this is being recorded.
Mom: Not true. She knows how to take selfies with it.
Can we focus, please? Question number 1. What is one of your favorite things we do as a family?
Melba: We cook, discuss recipes, gossip… no, I'm kidding, we don't gossip, we "share"—
Mer: Information about other people.
Mom: They're called "prayer requests."
Melba: We laugh, we listen, we give advice, and we

mean it. But I think my favorite is our holiday shopping trip, and that's saying something because I hate shopping! I think I mostly enjoy antagonizing each other in a locked-down car. No escape! Oh, and we get to eat out at fancy restaurants like Cheesecake Factory! Okay, on second thought, my answer is eat. I like it when we do that.

Mom: I like it when we cook together...

Mer: Yeah, the cooking is fun. We laugh a lot together and truly enjoy each other's company. We play games and travel, and there was that one time Melissa and Aunt Net got a couples massage together!

Melba: I'm sticking with *eat.*

Mom: I love it when we sing together; that is probably my most favorite.

Mer: Okay, I'm going with singing while we eat.

Mom: Now, *that's* a good answer. Don't you think that's a good answer, Melissa? Meridith always thinks through whatever she wants to say and so she always has a good response. They're clever, too, Meridith.

Yes, she's wonderful and the world would be better if we were all like her. Moving on!

Mer: Thank you for finally admitting that.

Melba: Here they go...

Question number 2. Do you have any life lessons that you would say you learned from one of us?

And if so, what was it and who did you learn it from?

Mom: I learned to never give Melba and Meridith any constructive criticism. They don't do well with that.

Melba: That is not true! And I'm offended that you even said it.

Mer: How dare you, woman!

Melba: The arrival of my daughter in my world taught me to better appreciate God's greatest gift, His Son. It's just that unconditional love that a parent has for their child, and the mercy that He allows for each day.

Mer: Oh, that's beautiful. Thanks, Mom.

Melba: That wasn't really about you, Meridith. It was about God.

Yeah, Meridith. You big dummy.

Mom: Melissa Paige. No, ma'am.

Mer: The lesson I learned was in watching Melissa's journey to become a mother. It was a lesson in patience, persistence, faith, mourning, hope, strength, and joy. I've lost someone I loved, but Melissa experienced a kind of loss I hope I never have to try to understand... the loss of a child. I watched her stand beside his tiny grave and cry. Then I watched as she waited for God to show His goodness. I never knew how good He could be, but I watched Him fill Melissa's home with two of the most beautiful children you've ever seen. Kids who could not be more like their mom and dad if they tried, in both actions and looks. God restored what was lost but gave them so much more in the end. It may not have been the timing they would have chosen, and I cannot imagine that it would have been the path they would have chosen, but the outcome was more than they could've asked for.

Melba: That's beautiful and I second it. I would toast to it, if you had made us any cookies.

Mom: Oh, Meridith, that was so well put. But as for you, Melissa, I'm sorry, I don't like getting on to you in front of your readers, but I just didn't like it when you called Meridith a dummy.

Oh my word. Let's keep going. Question number 3. How do you feel living in a family of strong women has shaped you?

Mer: Have you seen my shape? Y'all haven't helped. Believe me.

Melba: Yeah, what kind of shape are you talking about? Because I'm a circle.

We are talking about our insides here, people. Not our outsides. Y'all are too far gone for that.

Melba: We are steel magnolias, for sure. All of us. Because there are more of us that you aren't interviewing here today.

Mom: Our family is full to the brim of smart, strong, caring, funny women. So why did you just ask us?

Y'all are the only ones who agreed to come.

Mer: See? Our family is full of women smarter than us.
But in all seriousness, it makes me feel quite proud
and has shaped me in some great ways...but I've
also learned that this can be a bit of a double-edged
sword. Men were either threatened or turned off by
these qualities for years, so my dating life was super
boring; however, these just so happened to be the
qualities that initially attracted my husband, so
that was awesome! But in a marriage, these passed-
down traits can make it very challenging to submit
to your husband. Not that this is something my
husband requires of me...I just can't seem to shut
off the strong at times and let him take the reins, if
you know what I mean. I don't think that I'm alone
in this marriage hurdle, because I've watched the
women in my family struggle with finding the
same balance. We also have a very difficult time admitting when we are wrong and backing off of an
issue, so fighting in this family can be like a contact sport at times. Although, we will defend each
other to the death.

Melba: We exude a fragrance of love for one another,
enough love to speak the truth no matter what.
And we are beautiful, maybe not so much on the
outside—but on the inside, where it counts. We
are fragile enough to feel one another's pain, and I
have always loved that. We are strong in prayer for

each other, and we are fiercely loyal, even when we are mad at one another! People in town say we "circle the wagons" and keep it inside the family. We do! There's nothing wrong with that.

Mom: Melissa Paige, these are the most beautiful questions. I am so proud of you for coming up with these questions. You know who else would have probably come up with some beautiful ones?

Let me think... Meridith?

Mom: Absolutely she would've.

Mer: Thanks, Aunt Net.

Mom, answer the question!

Mom: I feel protected. I feel validated. I feel like if it's important to me then it will be important to them. If it worries me—it will worry them. I feel like when I'm strong it's because they have my back and would want that from me. And I feel like when I'm weak, they'll be my strength. I'm sad not everyone has that in their families.

(My Granny walks into the house.)

Mom: Oh, look who decided to join us!

Mer: Granny, what are you doing out of your house? You know it's five p.m., right?

Melba: And momma, the temperature isn't between seventy and seventy-two degrees outside. So, this is quite an adventure for you, isn't it?

Granny: Why don't you shut up? Every one of you.

I haven't said a word!

Granny: You're the worst of them all!

Granny, will you help us with these last few questions?

Granny: Probably not. But I'm going to sit here and there's nothing you can do about it.

Alrighty then, moving on to question number 4. When you look at our family, who is probably the bravest woman in it and why?

All of them at once: *Granny!*

Now, are y'all just saying that because she's sitting right here?

Melba: No. I'm saying it because she is!

Mer: She's tough as *balls*!

Melba: *Meridith Ann!* Don't talk like that!

Mom: Do you hear that, Melissa Paige? She is talking like you. She probably learned that from you and the way you talk!

Mom, the woman is thirty-six years old. She isn't a baby. I'm pretty sure she learned that all on her own!

Mer: Actually, I did hear you say it one day . . .

Mom: See? That really disappoints me. Your daddy and I did not raise you to talk about the private parts of a person.

Hey, Mer? Imma punch you in that face after this is over.

Mom: *Oh no, you're not!*

Melba: Granny is the strongest and the bravest, the
most independent, and probably the most misun-
derstood. She is an acquired taste for sure. I always
thought my dad was the strong one because he had
the muscle, but I see what he loved about her. Her
tenacious spirit, how she has prayed for her family
so fiercely for so long. But Melissa, even as much as
it pains me to say it, you are a close second.

Mer: I would agree. First, Granny. Then you. I want to
grow up to be brave like you, Melissa.

I'm still gonna hit you when this is over.

Mer: Fine, then I was lying. After Granny is my mom.
What I saw her do after my dad died? Now that
was strength.

Mom: In my mind, after Granny, would be Melba, too.
She lost her Donald at a pretty young age. But look
at her? Working hard, paying off medical bills,
raised two incredible kids who now have incredible
families. That's on her! She did that! One of the
strongest women I know.

Granny: I think she is brave. I think, Annette, you are
brave, too. You lost a child, and you fought
cancer—twice. You never let the world get you
down, and you always kept running to Jesus. When
Melba lost Donald I knew she would hurt forever
because I had lost my husband, too, and I knew
how it hurt. She was so strong, though, and she

would cry, and you girls would just hold her and I knew then that my family was tough and I was proud of that. But I think you all eat way too late at night. It's not good for your high blood pressure.

Mer: That was an awesome segue, Granny. Also, you didn't say anything about me or Melissa.

Granny: Y'all watch too much TV!

Okay, we are almost done. Question number 5. What has being around them, listening to them, cooking with them, fighting with them, and forgiving them taught you over the years?

Mom: There isn't really anything we can't work through. These women are worth the fight; good women almost always are. It's the fight and the forgiving that make us strong, you know that, right? I think that's what I would want everyone to know. Anyone can be bold and strong when everything is good. It's falling down in front of someone and having them extend an arm—not a criticism—that makes you better every time. For me, there has been a lot of falling down. But every time I got up I was stronger. And guess who helped me up?

Granny: The things that make you strong are the same things that could so easily make you bitter. You better choose which one you want to turn into. I could list you about ten women who made *the wrong choice*!

Mom: Mother, no.

Mer: Yes, Granny, do it!

Do you all think you are brave?

Melba: I think I'm brave because I get up every day, live my life, and keep my relationship with God as my primary source of strength. I could lie down and say, "I quit," but God has other plans for me! I refuse to give in!

Mer: To me, being brave means that you will face whatever comes with unrelenting determination. It applies to the single woman, as she sits watching someone else's wedding—I've been her. It applies to the barren woman, as she brings a gift to someone else's baby shower—I've cried with her. It applies to the sick woman, as she celebrates someone else's healing—I've prayed with her. I do consider myself brave, because I've walked into situations with an unflinching resolve that my circumstances would change. I once heard that you have to be brave with your life so that someone else can be brave with theirs. That is what the women in my family have been with me.

Mom?

Mom: I'm trying to be, baby.

Here we are! Last question. Describe each other in one word.

Mer: Oh no, this is going to end badly... But I would say Granny is hilarious, Mom is strong, Aunt Net is wise, and Melissa is gregarious.

Melba: Annette is a teacher, Meridith is loyal, Granny is
    independent, and Melissa, you are a dreamer.

Mom: That's beautiful, Melba. I would say Meridith is
    bossy, Granny is the grand dame, and Melissa is the
    master...

Really? The master? That's pretty awesome.

Mom: You didn't let me finish. You are the master-
    manipulator. You are a master at getting your way.
    That's nothing to brag about. Oh, and Melba, you
    are the warden.

Melba: What??

Mer: Oh, because of her hair?

Melba: What's wrong with my hair? And why would
    my hair make me a warden? Like, a prison warden?

Mom: Yes.

Melba: Can you explain that, please?

Mom: You just always are about discipline and you
    don't look good in anything tucked in.

Mer: Mom, you know this about yourself! The entire
    family voted you "Most Likely to Play a Female
    Prison Warden in a Movie."

Melba: I thought y'all were kidding!

**We weren't. Granny, would you like to describe me
    in one word?**

Granny: Pot-stirrer.

These are my girls. My family.

I call them chicken-fried women. They are women who may have been a bit battered on the outside, perhaps weathered, shaken, and bruised. Women who know that the real goodness, the most delicious part of us, never came from what was on the outside, but from the tender of our insides meeting up with the fight of our outside.

Women who don't burn when the oil is turned up.

Women who don't break when they're bent.

And women who figure—as most of the men in our lives can attest—that a little spice never hurt nobody.

I love you all, my chicken-fried women.

Melissa

Chapter 22

Look at These People, Kids. Your Mom Is Braver than All These People.

I got to the line at four thirty a.m.

It was forty-two degrees.

I was probably behind a thousand people who had gotten there earlier than me.

I stood in line behind a girl, in her twenties, who was perky and cute and practicing her guitar. Her name was Jane Ann, and she loved pink. She had a tattoo of the day she met her boyfriend. Oops, my mistake: her ex-boyfriend. She regretted the day she got the tattoo. She could yodel (personally, I think four thirty a.m. is a bit early to yodel, but maybe that's just me). She was going to sing an original song that she had written. Or maybe she would sing a Martina McBride song because it "showed off her chest voice." It didn't matter what she sang, her mother was proud of her. I know for two reasons:

1. Her mother was there with her in line... at four thirty a.m.
2. Her mother told me, "I'm so proud of her," once every five minutes. For five hours.

I told them my mother was also proud of me. Maybe. Who knows. She was tucked into her warm bed and completely unaware of the fact that I was standing in this line. Her mother tried to encourage me like she did Jane Ann, until we realized we graduated high school the same year. Then it was just weird.

Behind me was Tim. Tim wore all black and loved Nirvana. Tim sang like one of the Three Tenors—that was what was so intriguing about Tim. Well, that and he wore a top hat; I thought that was intriguing. A top hat, a Nirvana T-shirt, black skinny jeans, and Vans. His ears were pierced, and he had on exactly seventeen bracelets. I know because I counted. I had plenty of time to count. Tim was going to sing "Caruso" by Andrea Bocelli, and he was going to kill it. I heard him practicing and my jaw dropped. He came alone because he labeled himself a loner. Trust me, Tim: Tidy up the hair, lose the top hat, and just start singing, and I can assure you, you won't be a loner for long. I told him this and he said, "Yeah, that's what my mom always says."

His *mom*. That hurt.

They were Millennials.

I was middle-aged.

They wore athleisure wear.

I was wearing size 16 jeans with an elastic waist.

They brought Beats.

I brought my lipstick.

There was no confusing the generation gap between me and the rest of this here line, I will tell you that.

The doors opened a little after nine a.m. Two hours later I was auditioning for *The Voice*, a vocal competition I had never watched one minute of. I didn't really know what I was getting into, but it's not like that mattered. Chances were slim Adam Levine would be at this first round, but again, it's not like that mattered. What mattered was that it was January 9, exactly thirty-nine days since I had turned forty-one. Exactly thirty-nine days since I had made a decision to be brave.

The advertisement for *The Voice* auditions had come across my husband's computer one day. He walked in the room where I was sitting and said, "Do it."

"Do what?" I asked.

He showed me the banner ad and I snorted. "Uh, *no*! Been there. Done that. Got the T-shirt."

"That was a decade ago . . ."

"Emotionally scarred."

"It was a completely different thing..."

"Destroyed my self-confidence..."

"You said it was a year to be brave. You said you were going to risk things."

"We'll need to get there early."

I walked into the room, sang my song, and waited for the judge's ruling. Without embarrassing a single soul, without making people cry or turn to alcoholism, the judge politely thanked us for coming in and ushered every one of us out of the room, so the next fifteen auditions could come in.

I walked out of the room, took the escalator down, and walked out into the cold, gray Houston morning. I asked myself how I was doing, how I was feeling. I was smiling from ear to ear. I walked about a block back toward our hotel when I stopped to notice the line of people still wrapped around Minute Maid Park, awaiting their big chance.

I took out my camera. I turned it on video, pressed the red button, and then, in a video that to this day will be for my children's eyes only, I said these words:

Look, Remi! Look, Rocco!

Do you see all those people?

Look how many of them there are! They wrap all the way around the building! That's pretty crazy, huh?

You know what else is crazy? I came up here today

and stood outside with them. And you both know how much I hate being outside! But do you know why I did it? Because it is January 2015 and I am about to start living a year where I say *yes* to things that scare me. Where I say *yes* to things that make me nervous. Where I say *yes* to things that make me get up and get out and try. Where I say *yes* to things that make me uncomfortable.

Because how can I ever expect you both to try new and exciting things if I won't?

How can I expect you to be brave and courageous if I'm not?

So, take a long look at all those people.

(Oh, wait! Don't look at that guy. Oh jeez! I'm not sure what he was doing. Sorry about that, kids. Disregard!)

But do you see all the rest of those people? Your momma is braver than all those people. Every single one of them. None of them was as scared to come today as I was. But I don't want to be scared anymore.

It's going to be an awesome year!

I love you two, very very much.

I turned off the phone, slipped it back into my pocket, and began the walk toward the hotel. I checked in with myself again. How was I feeling? How was I doing? Did I want to throw myself in front of the oncoming public transportation? No. I didn't. I felt good. I felt brave. I felt like I had done something that I would not soon forget. I turned the corner and was about to head into my hotel when I saw Jane Ann—all pink everything—and her mom walking toward the parking garage. I waved.

"How'd you do?" they hollered.

"Great!" I said, "You?"

"I got a callback! So I'm going to celebrate and get a tattoo of today's date!"

I smiled and walked on.

God, I want you to make me brave...but there's a limit.

Chapter 23

When Hope Is Your Name (A Letter to My Daughter).

The first time I ever tasted your name in my mouth I was standing at the foot of your brother's grave. I stood there, for a long time, and stared at the stone that bore his name: Elisha. I stood in the cold February gray. I had left my coat in the car, which was fine, because I was mostly numb all over. My heart was not only broken, Remi, it was also jagged. You see, sometimes things break into smooth pieces. Other times, they hit the floor and land in jagged pieces that you can't see but that pierce you night and day until all of the mess is cleaned up. (Of course, that's the hard part—cleaning that mess up—and the process can take a very long time.) I remember that the wind started to blow and my hair started to whip about, and as it did I looked up and said the dumbest thing I may have ever said. I screamed it, actually...

"You owe me!"

You might wonder why those words were dumb. When something is given to us and then snatched away, we reserve the right to be repaid, am I right? We get to keep score. We hang on to our receipt and expect to be reimbursed in full. And at that moment, right there, at that grave, on that day, in that wind, I wanted my return on investment. What He had given, He had taken away. I wanted the score settled. I felt I was owed. And I told Him so.

But the truth was, God didn't owe me. He didn't owe me anything. Even with the loss of that sweet baby I had watched lowered into the earth, I had been given more than most will ever have. I had your daddy. I had my family. I had a home and friends and a coat that lay in the car. Yet there I stood. Numb and jagged and looking for a fight.

"You owe me!" I yelled, louder.

I was alive and I was standing my ground, on this very hill, in Tennessee.

"Do you hear me? I said, 'You owwwwweeee meeeee!'"

I began to cry after that, Remi. I began to cry

once I realized I was demanding repayment from a Father who had allowed me to get pregnant when I thought I couldn't. Who had allowed me to safely deliver a child some worried might kill me due to hemorrhaging. Who had given me moments with a baby that looked like me but lay still and gentle like your daddy. I screamed my rage at a God who had whispered things to me in my most broken moments; things that were so tender and kind that all I once was—lost and infertile and hopeless and angry—had washed away and what I was becoming was beautiful and whole and akin to hope.

And that right there, that moment, was the first time I ever uttered your name. *Hope.*

I knew that would be your name... were you to ever come.

Were you to ever exist.

Were you to ever be mine.

I felt my mouth form the word and I closed my lips around possibility. *Hope.*

I said it again. *Hope.*

Instantly the word caused me to withdraw my plea of payment. I felt remorseful, and as I plopped down on the ground, my head fell into my hands and I cried and apologized, and it took minutes for me to catch my breath.

Never was He angry. Only kind and gentle and patient. A presence that cannot be explained wrapped me up that day, Remi, and I was warm and cared for, and all the tears I shed that day—so many they could not be counted—became a medicine for me. A salve. A binding for my broken heart. I uttered your name a few more times and closed my eyes and, well, if I can be so bold as to say, I saw you. Long brown hair, huge smile, bright eyes.

My flesh wanted a boy—to replace my boy.

My heart and my soul and my God knew better.

You, Remi Hope, came to me sixty days later.

Hope has always been part of your name.

———

I wrote a chapter in this book about the night I turned forty-one. Someday you will read this book and you will read that chapter and you will know about one part that I left out. You are probably remembering it right now, aren't you? Many times I have closed my eyes and tried to push the memory away, but it always comes back. Sometimes those kinds of memories stay, as our reminder of why we did the things we did or said the things we said or changed the things we changed. It should probably stay our little secret, huh, Rem?

But why stop being honest now?

Always tell the full story, Remi Hope, always.

The night of my forty-first birthday I was just

finishing up putting dinner into the oven and you were watching television. The TV was loud and I had asked you to turn it down several times. You said later that you couldn't hear me and that was why you never lowered the volume, but that didn't matter. When I came to you, I came guns blazing. I walked into the room where you sat and where your brother lay on the couch, and I picked up the remote and threw it across the room. The batteries flew out and the remote fell in pieces to the floor. Your eyes widened and instinctively you placed your little hands over your ears and pulled your head to your chest. I screamed. I screamed and I screamed and I screamed, raging on about not doing your chores or not turning down the volume, that the table had not been set or homework was still not finished. Yet none of this—as shameful as it is—is what I remember most vividly. What I see when I close my eyes is you turning toward your brother and motioning for him to come to you. Arms open, you waved him into where you thought it would be most safe, next to you. You pulled him into your chest and you held on to him, tightly, until I had finished.

I did finish. With my throat hurting and my eyes stinging, I made my way to my bedroom, walked into my closet, shut the door behind me, fell to the floor and sobbed. I cried until I could not cry anymore. Which was about the time you opened up the door of my closet, calling out, "Momma? Momma? Are you in here?" I said that I was, and you came and curled up beside me, against my brokenness, against my jagged places, and there it was again: *Hope.*

"It's okay, Momma. It's okay. I'm not mad at you. I love you. Everybody has a bad day."

See? *Hope* has always been part of your name.

Years ago I began the process of writing a book. It was called *Dear Remi* and it was a story of how you came to be in my life. It was a story of how one severely broken person—played by me—can be given a gift so undeserved it takes your breath away— played by you. I still tinker around with it from time to time, but the truth is, that was not the story the world needed to hear. The story the world needed to hear was not the one I wrote *about* you, but the one I am writing *with* you. That is this story, Remi. That is *Eat Cake. Be Brave.*

This book is made up of a lot of stories from my childhood and my teenage years; it's made up of the choices I made and the hand I was dealt. There's laughter in this book and some sadness. There are stories and morals and butt-ins from your grandmother. But this book *is*—this book *exists*—because of you, Remi Hope. When you came into my life, bravery took on new meaning for me. I viewed things differently and I asked different questions. I wondered how, if I didn't do my part, you would deal with the fear you would someday face up to and the ineffectualness you would eventually succumb to. I needed you to see more than a broken woman crying in her closet. I needed you to see me as smart and capable, hardworking and feisty. I wanted you to watch me question things and seek out answers, attempt the things people thought I was ridiculous to try, feel beautiful in my own body, wear sleeveless on the cover...

Because I want you to be brave.

Lest we think that our only real power lies in our power, I also wanted you to see me fail. I wanted you to watch as I cooked it and burned it or as I wrote it and wadded it up. I wanted you to see me try and try and try until I finally stop, catch my breath, and admit that I will never be able to adequately perform hip-hop, so let's just move on. I hope you see me when I am frustrated. I hope you hear me when I have to give myself pep talks. I want you to see how I love and respect your daddy and how being tender and considerate toward him does not make me weak; it makes me happy. I want you to remember for the rest of your life that moment you caught me crying in the closet, because it goes to show you that sometimes a good breakdown is required for your life to change.

I want you to be okay with being vulnerable.

I want you to wear your red high-top Converse for as long as your little heart desires, even when I beg you to wear wedge sandals.

I want you to sit at the all-boys table in your fifth-grade homeroom because "they don't smell like perfume, Momma, they don't smell like anything... except maybe dog," even though there is a chair saved for you at the girls table.

I want you to continue being a zombie every single year for Halloween, even when I beg you to be a cheerleader.

I want you to buy magic sets with your Tooth Fairy money, even when I suggest a hairbrush or nail polish.

I want you to be the only girl on the all-boys basketball team and I want you to stand on the sideline and say, "Put me in, Coach! I've got to foul somebody or I'm gonna die," just like you did last week. (Your daddy was so proud.)

I want you to hold your arms out to your brother because he knows you are a safe place.

I want you to fight for the underdog.

I want you to question what doesn't sound right to you.

I want you to love Jesus and believe that when He says you can, you absolutely and without question *can*.

I want you to be you.

Maybe the book on how you came into my life will exist someday, but I'm okay if it doesn't. That would just be a story *about* you, and I am much more interested in writing a story *with* you. My life will never be the same since you screamed your way into it, Remi Hope.

Remi Hope.

Remi *my Hope*.

I am no longer jagged.

I fit together perfectly.

Thank you, for that.

With all my heart and all my soul, I love you.

Momma

Chapter 24

The Last Piece.

Here we are.

The last chapter. The last few words. The last time you will wonder why in the world your aunt Barbara bought this book for you for Christmas.

I think it's safe to say that everything in my life has a soundtrack.

My attempts at making the cheerleading squad were marked with "Eye of the Tiger" (not the Katy Perry one, but the eighties version that made you feel like no Russian stood a chance against you). I would try my jumps and my spins and my twirls and my kicks while listening to "Eye of the Tiger," but I would wake up on tryout morning...all three embarrassingly horrific try-out mornings...look in the mirror and mouth the words to Whitney Houston's "One Moment in Time."

Ohhhhh, my high school years. The soundtrack to those years were as embarrassingly sappy as you might imagine. I lay in bed and sobbed at Phil Collins singing about a groovy kind of love. I sang Debbie Gibson's "Lost in Your Eyes" at the top of my lungs, more than once. "Save the Best for Last" was the theme song of my high school crush. And to this very day, "Motownphilly" is on the list to play as people are leaving my funeral, which, let's be honest, will be quite the send-off.

My college years were filled with the soundtrack to *The Bodyguard*. I'd like to tell you there was other music, but pretty much, there was just Whitney and *The Bodyguard*.

Why do I tell you this? Because today, I am seated on my back porch and I'm laying down some Boyz II Men, "End of the Road," just for you.

Although we've come...

It's a fitting soundtrack.

We are here.

We made it.

If you are reading these words, then you didn't give up on this book—so it's kinda like you didn't give up on me, and I cannot thank you enough for that.

Maybe you picked this book up because you looked at the front cover and thought Cam from *Modern Family* had finally put a book out. Nope! Just me.

Maybe you bought it for a friend but ended up eating some bad oysters, so you chose to keep it for your most intimate bathroom moments.

Maybe there are a thousand different reasons why you chose this book, but all I care about is that you chose it. Or, it chose you. Whichever.

I'm glad this book made it into your hand. I hope, just as strongly, that it made its way into your heart. Once I was asked the question, "In ten years, where would you like to see yourself?" And I answered, "At a book signing for my new book—with a line wrapped around the building." I said that nine years ago. Please make my dream come true by coming out to see me whenever you get the chance. I have a feeling you and I would be good friends. How do I know this? Because I have shared with you some freakin' personal stuff in this book and you stayed. If that's not a sign of real love, I don't know what is.

Of course, there's another reason I want to see you, but just in case your kid gets a fever, your Match.com profile match decides you two should meet, you are working late again, or you are walking like a zombie around Trader Joe's, I will tell you what I want to say to you, right here, right now:

I would try out for cheerleader again and again and again.

I would stand in front of my seventh grade class and sing a country song.

I would stand in a line with 10 million Millennials.

I would stand up, speak up, or sing out.

I would face infertility.

I would face loneliness.

I would try and forgive and try again.

I would give birth and buy a casket and bury my heart.

I would do every one of these things again and again and again if it meant I got to take your hand and lead you into your new life of bravery. I would face every mountain, scale every fear, and climb every doubt if I knew that at the end of it I got to share it with you.

Listen to me, [your name here]: Life is too short to do the same dance to the same song every single day, year in, year out.

You weren't made to dance to one song.

You weren't made to sing only one verse.

You weren't made to eat only one piece.

You were made to live and live fully.

You can be scared—heck, we're *all* scared—but it won't be the boss of you anymore. It can't. You've come too far. Done too much. Prayed too hard. Listened too intently. The rest of what life has to offer is coming for you, and I want more than anything for you to walk directly into it screaming "Yes!" the entire time.

We've said no long enough.

Let's live now.

Really live.

So, the next time you have cake, think of me. Ten

bucks says I will also be somewhere eating a piece of cake. And not just because it's my birthday. But because it's a Tuesday or a Saturday afternoon or a balmy seventy-one degrees. I'll be eating cake because I want to. Because I'm celebrating. Because one day, a few years ago, I took a deep breath in, I held it for a moment, and I made a wish. And my wish was to be brave.

And she lived bravely, ever after.

Acknowledgments

I'd like to take a second and thank some people that are very important to me and that I love and appreciate very much but that, let's face it, probably won't make it into my Academy Awards acceptance speech.

Thank you to those of you who bought this book. Chances are you met me online ranting about my children or housework or facial hair and you followed me (literally and figuratively) and because you did it you gave me the confidence to continue doing what I love, which is making people laugh while wearing my pajamas. Until one day I made a little video called *Eat Cake. Be Brave* and it traveled all the way to an editor's computer in New York City and now you're holding this book in your hands. But if you didn't like me and you didn't believe in me and you didn't invest in my voice or my words then would that video have ever reached her? Would my words be down in print? I can't stand to think about it. So, you see why I am so thankful for you? You helped change the last half of my life. I would hug every last one of you if I could.

To the Social Squad: Someone asked me just the other day what the Social Squad was and I said, "A slumber party, an accountability group, a lifeline, a village, my friends. They are a cold Diet Coke and a hot bowl of queso... in other words, I guess I could live without them, but why in the world would I want to?" I'd like to stick with that description.

Thank you to TimberCreek Church for being home base for me. Man, I love walking through your doors! And to my pastor, my friend, my brother, Jeremy Yancey: The only thing you have done better than teach me—is Love me. You always told me I'd be doing this. It comes as no surprise to you.

To my Literary Agent, Terra Chalberg. Terra is my Literary Agent and she lives in New York because she is a Literary Agent. She is very tiny and smart and neurotic just like all the New Yorkers you see on TV... also, she is a Literary Agent. I have never had anyone work so hard on my behalf as my Literary Agent, Terra, I kid you not, she is relentless and she doesn't quit. And did I mention she is my Literary Agent? (This is apparently how many times I used the phrase "Literary Agent" when I first got one, according to my friends and family. I don't care, though! Because having one is awesome—but having one like Terra is a blessing.)

To my Editor, Beth de Guzman, and the whole Grand

Central Publishing team: The day I walked into our first meeting and saw that you had signed Chelsea Handler, Caitlyn Jenner, Stephen Colbert—and ME? I acted cool but I was dying! You said you believed in my "voice," and you've proven that. Thank you.

To the team who made the front cover and the back cover and the author flap cover happen: Kylie White (photography), Rob Fisher (hair), Ashely Conlon (make up), Grandough Bakery(cake). I went to the big city, then I came back home. And I'm so glad I did! I'm sorry I made y'all talk to me while I bathed.

To my assistant, Erin, who makes me think that she thinks that I hung the moon. Meaning, she doesn't really think that—but she makes me feel like she does, and really that is all I need. Thank you for saying no to all the jobs that have tried to hire you away with more money and less work in order to work endless hours with nothing to show for it. Also, please stop looking me directly in the eyes.

To Jaime Paxton-Morey. I wish that the world knew what you and I have up our sleeve! You are one of my most favorite things about this part of my life right now. I'm so glad it was me and not that girl with the really curly hair.

Friends are important to me. Which is why I wrote and re-wrote this thank-you a million times, because nothing I said felt enough. This might surprise you, but I'm a lot to handle. So to Karli, Janet, Ashley, Kelli, Rhonda, Kerri, April, Jen, Alexis, Katherine, Stephanie, Nicolle, Kristen, and Angela—these women who are doing life with me, and handling it all like a champ—I love you. I'm sorry I'm always late, I just didn't want to come.

To my family: my big, loud, Southern family. Y'all drive me nuts! Your group texts are going to send me to an early grave. And yet, you are the best part of me. You are what my children are thankful for each night at bedtime. You are what I am most anxious to be with when I've been away. You are matinees and dominos and Mexican food and swimming pools. We are so lucky to have one another, aren't we?

To Rocco: I'm sorry your sister got a whole chapter, but that's because you are a little shy and sometimes you don't like it when Momma talks about you in front of people. Rocco Cooper, you are *it*, son. You are just *it*, for me. When I look at you, I'm done. I can barely breathe. When I ask you to never marry and live with me forever I mean every word of it and your daddy is making me get professional help. I love you so much that I now have to talk to someone about it every Tuesday at four p.m.

And lastly, David Von. I don't think there has ever been another person that believed in me the way you do, except Christ. You are, without question, the greatest decision I have ever made.

My faith, my journey, my story is all due to "a friend that sticks closer than a brother." Everything I have and am and do is because of Him. If you have questions about Him then I would be so very honored to help make that introduction for you. You can email me at melissa@melissaradke.com.

About the Author

I was born and raised in the best place on Earth, a small town in East Texas called Lufkin. There was absolutely nothing to do on a Friday night so we would drive in circles around the mall until it was closing time and the police made us go home. I didn't care; I loved that town. Still do. It was there that I discovered the first real talent I had: singing. I sang for wedding and funerals, sweet-sixteen parties and Rotary meetings. I sang at a car show, a rodeo, and my high school graduation. After David and I were married I bought a really tight dress, put on a little Kenny G, and made his favorite meal because I had something very important to ask him...yada yada yada, it worked, and we moved to Nashville—where dreams come true and the four seasons are accurately represented!

I "graduated" (see chapter 16) from Belmont University with a Bachelor of Commercial Music Performance and a Minor in Jazz and Blues Music. I spent several years doing studio and session work for both Contemporary Christian and Country artists. I hated it with every fiber of my being. Like, I never ever want to do it again. Singing someone else's song? Someone else's words? Doing it someone else's way? Uh, no thank you. Mamma needs wide-open spaces.

In 2009 the Attorney General and I moved back to my hometown of Lufkin, near all my family and all of their loud talking and all of their hair issues. People ask me all the time why I moved back to Lufkin and I tell them the truth: Because the barbecue is better and the babysitting is free. We arrived with our two kids, Remi (12) and Rocco (9), who were both adopted after our million-year battle with infertility (see chapter 18). Our kids are very stunningly beautiful and outrageously funny and almost prodigiously athletic, like me. But then, at times, they are very sneaky, needy little creatures that require much supervision, like their father. In 2010 I became the Worship Pastor at TimberCreek Church and it was my most favorite job of all time (and I was once a secret shopper for Cinnabon...so that's really saying something!) but I had to leave it in 2017 when everything started taking off for me. Which was good because I was often reprimanded for my "lack of filter" and sexually explicit references to Channing Tatum.

But look at me now! Living my fanciest life on the

very thing my mom once said was "the end of the world as we know it": social media. I make videos and say things and contour my makeup for a following of, as of this writing, more than 330K across social media. The videos I've made, on Facebook alone, have had over 57 million views! Did you hear that? 57 million people have been—at one time or another—so bored that they watched me lament getting my first spray tan or attempt to French braid my hair upside down. Ten of my videos have gone viral and exceeded over one million views, with my "Red Ribbon" video being one of my most popular with over 100 million views across multiple websites and media outlets, not to mention during a university lecture in Phoenix, Arizona, which I still cannot understand.

I would just like to state for the record that I am not trying to brag about my videos going viral; it was just very important to my aunt Melba that y'all know about "my virility." This is what she calls it when we are at fancy places and she says, "Hey, Melissa, tell them about your virility." So, there, I've done it and now she's happy.

One of the things that I love the most is public speaking, and so for the last several years I have gotten the opportunity to travel all over the United States bringing laughter and encouragement to civic organizations, hospitals, schools, corporate events, churches, and women's gatherings. (But not one car show...weird.) You put me on a stage and tell me to make a bunch of people laugh?

I'm there! Recently, however, I have been asked to come and speak as a comedian and I'd like to set the record straight right here and now. I am no comedian. Just ask my kids.

I should probably also tell you that I recently signed with a television production company, Red Arrow Industries, to bring family-friendly entertainment to your televisions very soon. (I know, I know, and my mom thought social media was going to destroy the world.) My family and I just recently wrapped some of our first filming for the show and I have to tell you, you aren't going to see parenting this stellar anywhere else on TV. I'm not kidding; I'm pretty exceptional.

Which reminds me...does anyone know where my kids are?

No?

What about my car?

Lastly, I am supposed to tell you how busy I have been lately appearing on television shows, co-hosting radio shows, interviewing for magazines, newspapers, you name it. But it sounds like I'm lying, doesn't it? But I'm not! The last year and a half has been a whirlwind for me and some of the opportunities I've received I would never have even dreamed of. From appearing on daytime talk shows to being a topic of conversation for Robin Meade on CNN (Robin! Meade! Y'all!) and I am thankful for every bit of it.

The truth is, I worked hard for a lot of years in a town

where all sorts of dreams are supposed to come true, and yet they didn't for me. Only to move back to my hometown and have my whole world change. I think I've been preparing for this moment my whole life...I just didn't know it.

So there's your About the Author section. If you want to know any more about me please read chapters 1–24. Or you can wait for the tell-all book my kids will no doubt write someday. Just don't believe a word of it.